You Can't Make an Omelette Without Breaking a Few Eggs

I0225449

STEVE STANNARD

Publisher: Bob Selden
62 Ulysses Road RD10, Ashhurst
Palmerston North 4470
New Zealand
ISBN 978-0-6454956-9-0

National Library of Australia
Cataloguing-in-publication data:

Creator:	Stannard, Steve, author.
Title:	You Can't Make an Omelette Without Breaking a Few Eggs / Steve Stannard.
ISBN:	978-0-6454956-9-0 (paperback)
Subjects:	Community
	Business
	Decision Making
	Education
	Politics and Bureaucracy
	Health
	Environment
	History and Culture
	Self-Image and Positivity
Dewey Number:	010

Cover design by: Ben Odering, GSA Design
Cartoons by: Gwenda Saunders
Editor: Bob Selden

Contents

Foreword

It says plenty about Steve Stannard that his regular columns never sat beneath a catchy moniker.

No witty double entendre or matter-of-fact epithet was ever attempted to try and encapsulate the topic or tone of his op-eds in the Manawatū Standard. How could they? I never knew what he was going to write about and, to be fair, we never established what the parameters of his articles would be.

His occasional submissions in the late 2010s steadily hastened gradually and became a steady stream of insights and analysis by 2021.

"That story's not coming, what are we going to put on page 4?"

"A Stannard op-ed has landed."

"Think we ran that already."

"No, it's another one."

This was the common back-and-forth at the news desk, and Steve helped save "the daily miracle" on more than one occasion.

He was a rare breed as a contributor. It was common to have a roster of columnists who could each convey a perspective from an area of expertise be it politics, foreign affairs, the environment or fishing.

Steve was a scientist who ran a cafe and was heavily involved in the community through his passion for cycling. For me, that's a triple play; an academic, a small business owner and community stalwart all in one.

Importantly, he could also turn to his experience as a father, a husband, and an expat Aussie - and I loved that week to week I didn't know which "hat" he would be wearing.

It will be swiftly apparent as you tuck into *You Can't Make an Omelette Without Breaking a Few Eggs* that Steve devoured data and research-led evidence which guided his reasoning. The rationale he applied to scrutinising university grants and COVID statistics was just as effective -

and often more entertaining - when applied to weighing up whether home-baked scones or cans of Coke benefited his cafe more.

One might fear the scientist in Steve would mean his writing was dry or cold. It never was. His columns were conversational and thoughtful, with a strong awareness of who his readers were; everyday Kiwis.

He didn't fire from the hip, he was not inflammatory and rarely courted controversy. He was considered and a bit crafty - deftly calling on analogy and allegory to connect his eye for detail to the bigger picture. Enjoy how he could spend 500 words detailing a specific example or anecdote, and then with a sentence or two reveal how he was discussing the economy, the health system or our collective human nature all along.

Steve's articles could be a right bugger to "sell", by which I mean to headline and synopsise for a homepage and social media sharing. To try and sum up his columns bore the risk of spoiling the reveal.

If I was to attach a name to the series of columns Steve wrote for the Standard, in retrospect, I would cheekily suggest Where Is He Going With This? That is what I was often thinking when editing his wonderful words.

And the answer would always be the same: Somewhere satisfying.

Matthew Dallas

Editor of Manawatū Standard

Tuesday, February 18, 2025

This is a compilation of short articles I have written for the media, almost exclusively whilst living in New Zealand.

Apart from one or two, they have all been published in either the Post, Stuff.co.nz, the Manawatu Standard, or the NZ Herald. This means that they have been through a peer-review process, which as a former academic, is important to me.

They are primarily Opinion Pieces, but unlike many other such labelled published articles by others, I try to back many of these up with evidence, often data. Again, that's my academic background coming through!

If they are not driven by data or other "evidence" then often they describe a personal experience, often borne of frustration. Personal experience makes an article less dry, and tells you something about myself.

In fact one of the reasons I decided to create this compendium was to share to the world a little about me. I guess it means I don't have to write an autobiography!

Finally, very often I have felt a little restricted by what I can say in these articles because it might not fit within the narrative of the masthead.

So, on many occasions I have tried to leave a subtle message that the reader has to identify by thinking hard about the words. That has been a skill for both myself and will be for the reader to be able to get the full message!

While that might all sound a bit dry, I hope the articles are either entertaining or informative.

The people who are the inspiration for putting this book together include author Bob Selden, who somehow sees some value in my writing! But also the many people who encouraged me to write and publish over the years, sometimes because they have felt constrained to do the same thing. Lastly, many people that have told me that I have encouraged them in some way with what I have written over the years.

Steve Stannard

For Elizabeth, Robert and Thomas.

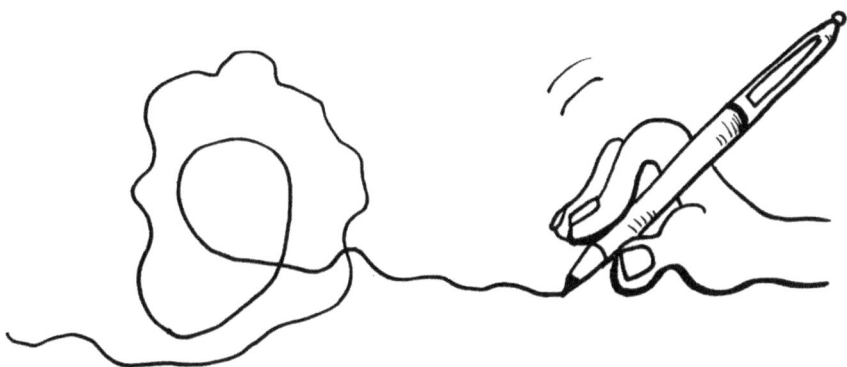

Community

Christmas Letter to a Neighbour

Inclusion – who's selected to be "included"?

Christmas Letter to a Neighbour

Hi neighbour; season's greetings! I really should pop by for a chat, but I thought I'd go for the long-winded New Year's letter because we don't cross paths that often these days. Anyhow, seasons greetings to your wife and the kids too.

Been meaning to tell you how much I love your new double cab ute. Blood red with orange flame decals on the side, my favourite colour scheme! The "Eliminator" model I guess? I was told it was a special edition named after NZ's COVID response.

How long have you had it now, a couple of months?

I see you got a bit of work done on it to raise the height. Are you parking it outside now because it doesn't fit in the triple garage? Although I know you have a jet ski, the wife's RAV and the Commodore SS in there, so that's probably why you need to park across the footpath. Hardly anyone uses footpaths these days, so no worries there mate.

Anyway, as a rate-payer, you're entitled to use the road, verge, or footpath to park your car aren't you?

And if any little old ladies walking on the footpath wanted to get around your beast they can walk into the road. They obviously aren't paying road user charges like you and me.

Those flared guards with the big wide tyres are pretty smart. I read somewhere that they were there to make it more stable in the deep mud. Or on the beach when you are dodging those pesky families sitting under their beach umbrellas. Bet you're looking forward to tearing up and down some of those sand dunes over the break!

Must be great driving the beast around town where you can look down on everyone else, aye? Feeling so safe that if you were in an accident you'd be fine even if the other car was completely flattened.

I guess you don't need to worry about where the gutter is when you park downtown for a coffee either? It certainly makes a statement when you park it right outside the café on Sunday mornings where you go for brunch. I'm sure everyone admires it and of course that means that they admire you as well.

Did you get the six spotlights, bicycle rack, and kayak holder with the car or did you put them on yourself? Reeks of a man of action, which you obviously are, although I've not seen you actually ride a bike, or paddle a kayak yet. Got to be prepared though aye just in case Santa comes to the party.

Not sure about the number plate though bro', 'RUNUOVA'. Some sensitive soul might take a dim view of that, so you could change that to something like "MINESBIGGA", "CO24EVA" or "ROADKILL". Might upset some of the greenies, but you work hard, pay tax, and deserve a big ute and number plate to suit if you want one. And the latter name is really in tune with the colour scheme.

The beauty of the dual cab model is that it was designed specifically to take the kids to school. You know they are going to be safe during that epic one km trek to the classroom from your place. Those poor kids whose parents make them ride to school will have to give way to you that's for sure. And your kids won't miss class anytime soon when you drop them right at the front gate. They'll be proud as punch being dropped off in your massive machine.

With the big tray at the back your missus will be able to get the weekly shopping done in one fell swoop! And when the boys come around for the next test match, picking up three or four cartons is a cinch.

I'm wondering though whether it's a work car or not? Being an accountant, I guess you have to visit a few people with gravel on their driveways, so the 4x4 and ten-speed automatic gearbox will be super handy. Anyway, anyone who's anyone has a ute as a work car because you just never know when all that grunt and grip is going to be needed.

Anyhow, all the best for the New Year. Enjoy your well-earned break and we'll catch up for a few cans at some point.

Best, your neighbor.

PS. Seems the same mud spray has been on your ute for the last four weeks. It looks great but let me know if you want a hand washing it off.

Inclusion –
who's selected to be "included"?

The Tokyo Olympics start in a few weeks. It looks like most of our athletes will do a fly-in just before their event and fly-out just after their event to minimise any chances of getting or spreading the Covid virus.

I feel really sorry for them, missing out on the Opening Ceremony, the goings on in the athlete village, and then the Close. It's those special extras that make it the once-in-a-lifetime experience it normally is. Most have trained for many years to get there. But at least they are still going to compete at their pinnacle event on the world stage. And they will still be Olympians, still the very select few.

Being the select few means they have met certain criteria. These are primarily performance-related and quite specific for individual events called an 'A' standard. For team events, it is usually a world ranking from a series of prior competitions.

Sometimes there are more capable athletes than are able to go because a country can have only so many spots in an event.

In the blue riband men's 1,500m athletics event, for example, we have two spots, but we have more than two who could make a semi-final at least.

That's how selective, how exclusive the Olympic Games are - you can be that good and still not get the gig.

In contrast to the 1,500m, NZ doesn't have an athlete or team good enough to meet the criteria in most Olympic events. Our team has 199 athletes including some large teams, but there are 339 different events. We have no one in the majority of the swimming and athletic events. No one in synchronised swimming, diving, handball, volleyball, basketball, or surfing. Then there's taekwondo, judo, and archery.

The selection criteria are so stringent because the Olympics are about only the best competing for their country on the world stage. It's about exclusivity. It's excluding the vast majority of athletes so that only a very few can compete.

That's what makes the Olympics such a big deal. That's what makes it interesting, and that's what makes it the biggest sporting event on the planet every four years.

Even getting involved as a non-athlete in the IOC is exclusive; you have to be well-connected, ski in Switzerland, and own a large yacht.

So it's interesting that "The IOC is committed to inclusion across the Olympic Movement".

The context of this is their wish "to develop guidance to help ensure that athletes – regardless of their gender identity and/or sex characteristics – can engage in safe and fair competition".

Putting the vexed transgender debate aside, it does seem ironic that the most exclusive organisation in the world can all of a sudden say it is "inclusive".

It appears that the IOC think that "inclusion" only relates to gender and/or sex. I am hoping it also means skin colour, socio-economic status, level of education, political persuasion, religion, and other such beliefs. Where does the inclusiveness stop?

If they really want to be inclusive maybe they should include people who don't meet the A standard? Me for starters. I've always wanted to run the 100m in front of a billion TV viewers.

Perhaps they should also have age categories, starting with the under twelves. Otherwise it's age discrimination isn't it? Or weight categories in all events. It'd give skinny people a chance in the shot-put.

And the current Olympic movement excludes other animals except horses. I'm sure dogs are itching to get involved.

Ah, so the IOC is being exclusively inclusive! Or they are using the word "inclusive" to demonstrate that they agree with an ideology that 'inclusive' now represents. That's fine, but let it be acknowledged that the IOC only exists in the first place because of its exclusionist nature.

Perhaps they are confusing the ideas of "equal opportunity to compete" and "inclusiveness"?

Anyway, I'm looking forward to some hours watching the telly, seeing Kiwis battle the rest. I don't care whether they win or lose. Just the fact that they did the hard yards to get an invite to the most exclusive gathering on the planet gets kudos from me. That's gold.

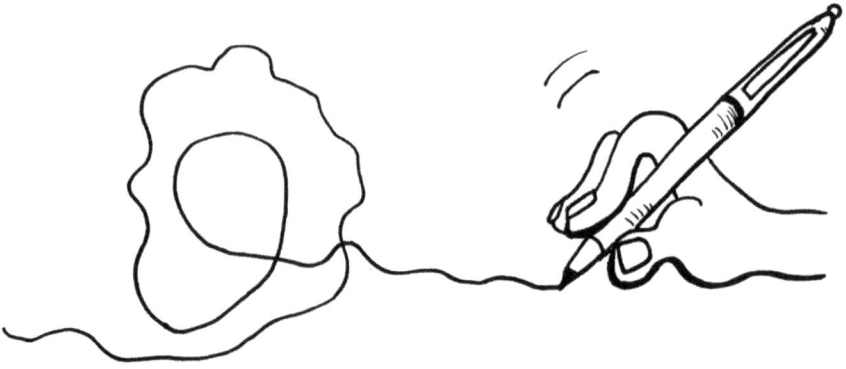

Business

Starting something new, like lighting a fire, is mostly about good preparation

Making our country more productive – but how?

The Change Managers: Paratroopers who drop in, shit everywhere, and then piss off!

They paved paradise, (and) put up a (supermarket) parking lot

Sneaking the sunrise past the rooster

You can't make an omelette without breaking a few eggs

Starting something new, like lighting a fire, is mostly about good preparation

There's nothing like sitting next to a roaring fire on a cold winter evening, cup of tea and book in hand.

It's a privilege to have a wood fire in the modern world because there are plenty of places now where this old-fashioned way of domestic heating is not permitted.

However, having a fireplace is one thing, and having a decent fire in there is another. That's because lighting and maintaining a good fire is not easy.

In a perfect world, you start off with some whisper thin super dry kindling placed on top of some newspaper. Strike a match first go, light the newspaper and, hey presto, the fire roars to life. The inferno is then sustained by a tinder-dry woodpile matured over the recent endless summer.

The reality, however, is different.

You can't just go outside and find some suitable kindling in the garden when you want it because when you finally decide it's cold enough to light the fire, it's dark and probably damp. Or the little stack you had made up over summer has already been exhausted.

You find some newspaper anyway, and some bigger sticks you break up and set it all up in the firebox. The quality of modern matches are so poor that the first four match heads crumble during the strike. Finally, on the fifth go you get a short-lived and tiny flame on the matchstick which you quickly apply to the newspaper.

The sticks you arranged under which the newspaper is placed, don't seem to want to catch fire, so, you keep feeding newspaper in until you've used the equivalent of Saturday's Post.

When the sticks finally light with some assistance from a few big breaths, billows of smoke escape into the living room. The only thing to do at that point is to open all the doors and windows to get rid of the smoke, thereby letting all the cold air in.

At some point you decide that the fire is going to kick on and so you fiddle with it by carefully placing a couple of larger pieces of wood on top. Instantly, the fire collapses and only a few feeble flames remain; if you are lucky.

Only another weekend newspaper, plenty of blowing, and billows of smoke gets it going again. Finally, the larger bits of wood light up and you can walk away, for a while at least.

After an hour or so, just as the room is getting nice and warm, it's nearly time to go to bed.

And this, dear reader, is why people buy heat pumps.

Getting a fire going is an art. It needs good preparation, skill and experience, patience, and knowing when and how to intervene.

And there is a critical point in that process of lighting a fire when you know, from experience or intuition, whether it's going to kick on or not.

I reckon lighting and maintaining a fire is a good analogy of starting and running a business. Getting it going requires preparation, knowledge, and ideally experience. And a spark.

Once it's up and running, knowing when to intervene is crucial. You need to make sure that it doesn't run out of fuel on the one hand, or collapse because it's been fiddled with too much on the other.

I will go further and suggest that it is also a good reflection of how the NZ business economy should be managed. The mob down in Wellington need to be able to lend enough support to struggling businesses so they can fire up, be productive, and value-add. At the same time they should not fiddle too much with those parts of the business economy which are burning brightly and keeping NZ "warm".

A short-sighted policy maker though, would simply go out and buy a heat pump made in China.

Making our country more productive - but how?

In exercise physiology we talk about efficiency in terms of movement. It is defined as the amount of external work done per unit energy that is expended.

For example, an efficient cyclist will go farther along the road than an inefficient one for the same amount of energy used. Provided, of course, all other things like bikes, body size, speed, and road surface being equal.

If we think about motor vehicles, broadly a more efficient engine will enable a car to go further than a less efficient one for the same energy content of fuel that goes into it.

In reverse, a car or other bit of machinery which is inefficient, can expend vast amounts of energy and perform little external work. That is, there is little gain to show for the energy or effort that is put in. Think of sitting at a set of traffic lights with the car engine running.

People can be efficient or inefficient too. In fact, we are often told by economic 'experts' that we Kiwis are inefficient workers. That is, we produce relatively less good or product than other nations for the same level of work that we do. And that, apparently, is why our wages are low.

According to a 2016 report by MBIE, we have, "High numbers of hours worked, high employment and favourable policy settings which predict that incomes should exceed the OECD average by 20 per cent. But New Zealand's income levels are more than 20 per cent below the OECD average".

In other words, most of us spend long hours at the workplace and we should get paid well, but we don't because we are not efficient.

So why are we inefficient? It's something I've thought much about and asked many people about to try to get an idea because it impacts on what we as a country can spend on health and education.

The explanations that MBIE give are:

• *The small size of the economy and distance from world markets.*

• *A firm size structure where very large (productive) firms are scarce.*

- *Relatively low levels of investment in business research and development.*
- *A high relative cost of capital, with high average long-term interest rates compared with other OECD countries.*
- *(And finally) Low levels of competition in some parts of the economy.*

Some of these things, like the fact that we are at the arse-end of the world, we cannot change. And our population will never be that of similar-sized Japan, I sincerely hope.

At an individual or small/medium business level, all of these MBIE explanations are beyond our control, so how can we, as individual workers and small business owners help make NZ more productive, with around the same amount of input?

From my perspective as a small business owner this comes down to improving day-to-day work-related efficiency.

Think of those endless meetings where there are no tangible outcomes, except another meeting next week. Or the increasing number of hi-vis vest-wearing people walking around aimlessly at road-work sites. Lengthy consultation processes where the outcome is already pre-determined. Management by paper-based policy sent via email which just gets ignored. People in management positions that just create work for themselves by mandating any of the above. High staff turnover (churn) which decimates institutional knowledge. And of course, losing your best worker to greener pastures (or Sydney).

Worst of all is when government introduces some big initiative requiring a whole lot of minions to do massive amounts of work, but then reactively reverses or changes that initiative because of a bit of external pressure. This naturally happens when governments change, and in NZ our three-year election cycle means that it happens more frequently than elsewhere.

One of the things I learnt from the sport of cycling is that you need to be always concentrating on where you are in the peloton so you can save every ounce of energy, so you can be as efficient as possible. It means that you will have more energy left when it gets hard towards the finish. Look after the joules and the kilojoules will look after themselves.

For my little café business, gains in efficiency include; riding my cargo bike into work to avoid petrol and parking costs, looking for specials when buying food, regular self-servicing of equipment where I can, and minimizing food waste through flexibility and timely preparation.

We should all be thinking about how we can be more efficient in our workplace, not just for us as individuals or our small business, but also for NZ going forward.

Because we need to be going forward at a time where the country seems to be stuck at the traffic lights while the engine is still running.

The Change Managers:
Paratroopers who drop in, shit
everywhere, and then piss off!

Some 17 years ago we bought our house in Palmerston North from an elderly couple who built it around 1960. It's a very well built house with a large established garden, both of which were carefully constructed over some four decades and lovingly kept. Apart from the retro décor, one thing I immediately liked were the little additions the (handy) man of the house had designed - a shelf here or cupboard there, the walk-in pantry, garden drainage, and even multi-coloured plastic fly strips in the doorways. It sort of reminded me of my upbringing in the 70s in Sydney.

But my wife did not reminisce in the same way, moving straight into demolition mode, doing away with the pastel colour scheme and patterned carpet. Making her domestic "mark" I guess, based on her preference, trends, and not having to ask a landlord.

However, a full four seasons in the house and kids running around exposes the human stresses and environmental strains of living in a particular place. Only then the reasons for our handy man's work became clear. His additions were done cleverly, in reaction to experience, time living in the house, and with plenty of thought.

And so it is in business.

These days there is an occupation called 'change manager'. This is a person who is parachuted into a business by the top brass with the mandate of improving it.

They are usually guided by the increasingly important (and seemingly more powerful) bean counters driven by an annual bottom line, not quality, reputation, or opportunity.

The problem with change managers are that they are never there long enough to survey the business to see where efficiencies can be gained. And then after making changes, they are not there long enough to see whether these have worked.

Most of us who have worked in big institutions in recent years can describe one of these "paratroopers" who have fired, hired, changed the brand of communal tea bag, and then left a trail of destruction behind. They head off back across the ditch for their next six-month job after being paid more than the sum of the people who have been fired. Change managers have no skin in the game.

I've never actually seen a change manager who has dropped in, considered their new destination, and then said, "Well actually, you've got a good group of staff and things are running fairly well – there is little I can do...". Of course, no one would pay their handsome fee for information like that! In fact the more change they make the more valuable they are surely!? So, they have to at least centralise the internal services, get rid of a layer of middle management, and send the nice lady who answers the phone to Calcutta.

But 17 years, including 15 proper summers (two were duds) in our house has taught me that just coming and changing things for the sake of change shows scant regard for those who came before, who were just as intelligent as you or I and had made decisions for a very good reason. Sure, the environment changes, and sometimes people are rigid in their thinking, so changes in the way a business runs are required. Sometimes there needs to be a change in organisational structure, or sometimes what's on the shelf does need new packaging. The point is, change needs to be done in a very considered manner because the people coming before did things primarily for a very good reason at the time. Like our handyman with his wealth of 'institutional knowledge' about our home.

Patterned carpet is coming back anyway, and I've squirrelled away a set of those coloured door strips just in case.

They paved paradise, (and) put up
a (supermarket) parking lot

I shop at supermarkets. I visit one every day on my way to my little café. Each morning I pick up the milk, cream, bananas, and other stuff I need for my shop.

Most often I'm riding my special cargo bicycle which can carry a small kitchen sink, albeit slowly, so half a dozen 2L bottles of milk and some bread is a manageable load. However, sometimes the weather is so bad I have to drive – like everyone else – and park in the paved expanse which defines a supermarket carpark.

A supermarket is a one-stop shop where you can buy all the things you need at the one place. Apples to zippers, probably. Beetroot to yoghurt certainly.

You don't need to write a shopping list when you shop at a supermarket, you can just walk up and down the aisles and fill the trolley with things that clever marketing campaigns convince you that you need. These days you can even refuel with an espresso and cake once you've checked out.

With their size and appetite for stocking just about everything a consumer needs, supermarkets are the pinnacle of our food chain. And being chains or franchises controlled by large publicly listed companies, these big boys hold all the cards when negotiating with suppliers. They have serious commercial grunt, and accordingly, political clout.

Maybe that's why these places and their workers were considered "essential" during the Covid lock-down when our local butchers, bakers and candlestick makers were hung out to dry.

But when you think about it, more than half the stuff a supermarket sells is not essential. In fact once you've passed the meat/vegie part of the store, there's not much other food you really need except maybe milk and bread (and peanut butter, my favourite). Anything they sell that's not food you can purchase at either the pharmacy or hardware store, or it's not worth buying.

For example, soft drinks in various guises take up one whole aisle of your average supermarket, that's maybe 10% of the floor space. Sugar-filled breakfast cereals and shampoo/conditioner/moisturisers - the same. Then there's the large alcohol section. Nice "to haves", but not essential.

Anyhow, once you've done your weekly shop at Pak-N-Save or Woolworths you need to carry it home. Cue the motor vehicle.

The bigger the supermarket, the more customers, and the bigger the carpark. I'd be willing to wager a decent sum that there is an algorithm, known only to supermarket designers, that tells you how big the carpark has to be according to the EFTPOS turnover.

Over time supermarkets have become bigger as they've consumed the smaller retailers and taken over their traditional inventory. Accordingly, supermarket carparks have become so big that they have their own petrol bowsers, in case someone runs out of petrol while they're cruising around looking for that parking spot closest to the front door.

And what would happen if we didn't have cars, or we ran out of petrol? Then we wouldn't need supermarket carparks! And it follows that supermarkets wouldn't exist.

Instead you'd have a couple of hectares of city or suburban land you could use for a park, housing, or a collection of small shops selling truly essential items. Butchers, bakers, green grocers, all with produce sold fresh or processed on the premises. Not from a far-off factory from where logistics and transport require chemical preservation and layer upon layer of packaging.

You'd pop into one of those little shops knowing you need their stuff because that's what they specialized in, and maybe to have a chat with the owner whom you would see regularly.

No duopolies in town either, but true competition. The shoppers' paradise!

And if you really needed a coffee, you'd go to a proper café. You could walk to the shops, ride, or catch a bus because you didn't have to carry all that stuff you didn't need.

In fact, once upon a time that's how it used to be, when our life didn't revolve around cars.

But then they paved paradise, (and) put up a (supermarket) parking lot.

Sneaking the sunrise
past the rooster

When I was told that my recent article on the city Ring Rd ruffled a few feathers and put a few car-centric locals into a flap, I thought of chickens. Not whether they'd cross the Ring Rd, but why we have chicken-related idioms and phrases in our vernacular.

One summer long ago, as a twelve year old, I caught a wild rooster and took him home. Assuming he was lonely, I borrowed a couple of hens from a friend of mine and then proceeded to grow my own flock.

My teenage years were spent, amongst sport and school, tending the chickens in the morning and then again in the afternoon. I was proud to be able to take a handful of fresh eggs to the kitchen for cooking and baking.

Many an hour was spent watching them and understanding how they went about their business, how they behaved.

Chickens are social animals. They prefer to hang around in groups, and they get lonely on their own.

They have a hierarchy. If you have a rooster he's the top dog, the Chairman of the Board. He literally rules the roost at night, and during the day he spends his time keeping his flock safe by rounding them up now and again so that he knows where they all are. His other main jobs are to ensure his hen's eggs are fertilised, and that his humans get up at the crack of dawn. If there's another rooster the two of them will fight. Viciously. Roosters are almost comical to watch strutting their stuff, but they take their important position very seriously.

Hens really do have a pecking order, and if there is no rooster, it's pretty nasty. Through intimidation and some argy-bargy, the order is set, and you don't want to be on the bottom. Down there you have to wait to eat after the others have finished, and you are always on your toes trying to avoid getting verbally and physically assaulted. At the bottom of the pecking order, you don't share the lofty heights of the upper perch, so you can literally get shat upon. One lowly-ranked hen we had found an outlet by picking on the cat. The cat probably responded by kicking the dog.

Chooks love roaming around the yard and when they can do that, boredom is released and the social pressures dissipate. Anyway, it's easier to run away from the bully when you're not locked down in the chicken run.

Outside they are constantly scratching around to find healthy food; grubs, worms, green leaves, carefully tended vegetables, and cat food. Cats are no match for a hungry chicken. There's a reason why the chooks aren't let out in a Japanese garden, but then again backyards with chooks don't have a snail problem.

If one hen is given something big and yummy then it will run away with it in its beak, the others chasing until the lucky one drops her meal or the pursuers become distracted. If they think one of their peers is onto something good, like a newly planted patch of garden, they'll jump on the bandwagon. And trendy places where they can scratch around or dust-bath can be popular all summer until one day it's suddenly forgotten.

When hens are stressed they stop being productive. If they get frightened or you move them to an unfamiliar place they will stop laying for a few days until they can become accustomed to their new environment.

The worst is when you put a new hen in with the incumbents. There will be merciless agitation and bullying until a new pecking order is established and relative calm then descends.

If you don't collect the eggs for a few days, one will get clucky and stay on the nest. Three weeks later, if the rooster is competent, some fluffy chicks will emerge. Mother hens spend their days keeping the chicks under their wings, and "helicoptering" their brood. Other hens won't mess with a mother hen because they will fiercely protect their chicks and will occasionally give a rooster the hurry up.

All sounds rather familiar doesn't it? Humans are more like chickens than we'd like to admit. Even this rooster. They are a parody of us and so are part of our language.

For example, when some dumb cluck ruffles my feathers by feeding me some cock and bull story I try not to brood over it. Instead, I'll hatch a plan to write something which will put egg on the face of that bird brain. Being no spring chicken, I'm disinclined to walk on eggshells to get my point across, but then getting it past the editor can be like sneaking the sunrise past the rooster.

You can't make an omelette without breaking eggs

I get up at 5 am or earlier, seven days a week, to do the daily baking for our café. Muffins, scones and biscuits usually, as my wife does the slices in the evenings.

The other morning we had an order for a dozen muffins to fill on top of the usual amount, so I knew I was going to go through a few more ingredients than usual.

I always do a bit of preparation the night before, but this time I forgot to account for the extra eggs needed.

Now, usually we have enough from our backyard chickens topped up with some free-range from the supermarket. But when I started my daily baking ritual early next morning to make the extra muffins, I knew I was going to be in trouble.

So, there's me at 5am rummaging around the nesting boxes in the chook pen looking for eggs. Nada.

When this sort of egg supply issue occurs, my first point of blame isn't me for not buying an extra dozen – I'm the big boss so it's never my fault. The fault is with chicken management.

The rooster is always crowing that he's in charge, so I had a word to him. He looked me strait in the eye and you could see Foghorn saying, "Not my fault buddy. I can do lots of chicken things, but laying eggs isn't one of them". But I was pretty sure he'd have words to his crew a bit later.

He did, but as far as I could understand all Foghorn did was crow – again - that he was in charge. And when I let him out he just wandered down to the fence to show off to the hens next door.

So later on in the day I went around Foghorn Leghorn middle management and told the hens straight to their beaks that unless productivity improved that I was going to sharpen the axe.

I guess the 'stick' approach is not the best way of encouraging improved production in the chook pen, but I was angry and serious. I'm expecting that one of the hens will write to the egg layers union (ELU) complaining about my bullying behaviour.

They might also complain to the ELU about a lack of insulation in their coop. Who knows, the hens might demand under foot heating in the nesting boxes or better ventilation in the coop. Bah humbugs!

I could instigate a complete restructure I suppose. After all, restructures are all about getting rid of workers aren't they? But imagine the squawking that would go on then! And another one of the hens will write to the ELU complaining about the loss of jobs.

Perhaps management could do with a change? Foghorn needs to keep his eye on the job better and spend less time wooing the ladies next door. After all, I don't get the pickings from their nests. He'd be a big part of the restructure. I could demote him to Health and Safety, but then what sort of example is he going to set each night when he goes to the top of the perch without a harness?

I know other owners who have temporarily imported a change manager, always an older bigger hen who rules the roost, and bullies and cajoles the others onto a lower perch. Then you return them after a bit so that the current crop of hens restructure to a new pecking order - if the most productive ones have not flown the coop by that point.

The easiest thing to do would be to close down the business, get rid of the whole lot of them. I would pay two days' chook food as a redundancy package and sell them on Trade Me.

It's not my business if they end up in a pot somewhere, because me the primary shareholder, would be happy with the short-term return. And going forward I could always just import 100% of my eggs from the supermarket.

Supermarket eggs aren't nearly as good, of course. No nice golden yolks, and fresh from the hen eggs make a superior muffin. That's why our muffins have a good reputation.

No chook poo for the garden either, or a means of recycling our food waste from the café. Oh well.

But I'll still have the infrastructure, the hen house, which has a book value. Most importantly, my name is written and dated in the concrete floor of the coop. It's there for future generations to admire, even if there's no productivity emanating from the coop.

It's getting hard to see my name etched in the concrete though, because it's covered in chook poo.

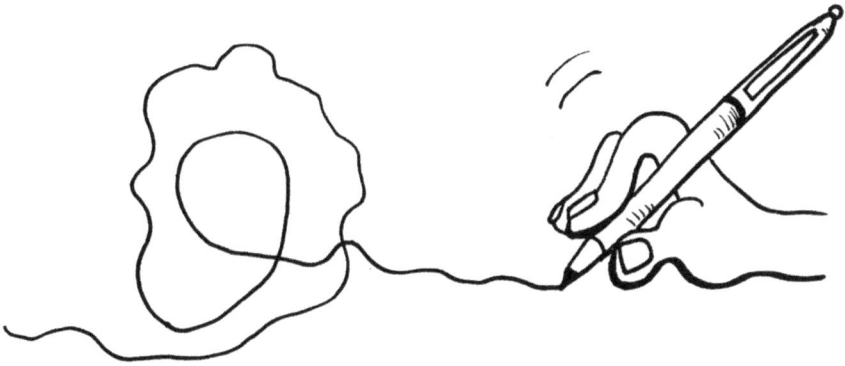

Decision Making

To be or not to be?
That is the question

Academics are a passionate lot. Some, though not all, are passionate about teaching, but all are passionate about the research that they do.

Research is an essential part of an academic career because possessing the latest knowledge means that, in theory at least, they can impart that cutting edge to their students. Research also gives their university 'profile' and ideally an external (non-university) income source. Anyhow, if it's in their job description they have to do it.

For many academics finding time to conduct research is difficult given the teaching load and ever-increasing administrative duties. But their passion for creating knowledge in their chosen area of research and a conviction that it is important will drive some to do many extra hours of work. Even if that research is very esoteric, or from a bystander's point of view, useless.

Some more than others, but by and large, NZ academics work hard.

So, when an academic's research expertise gets noticed it's like Christmas. A newspaper report or better still, a TV interview, gets a pat on the back from the university marketing machine and more fodder for next year's promotion application.

Most academics, of course, spend their careers plugging away in the lab or at the desktop, and never get noticed. But sometimes something happens – an earthquake, political upheaval, or a pandemic, and they make the front page as the resident know-all about that event. They get their 15 min of fame and then slide back into obscurity hoping for another *coup de-etat* or variant to emerge. But there are some who get a taste for public attention and don't recognize when their 15 min is up.

With a few exceptions, the modern NZ academic engages in very focused areas of research which few others, sometimes only other academics, can appreciate.

However, being an expert in that narrow area doesn't mean you are expert at anything else. In fact, given that there are only 24 hours in a day and only seven days in a week, being an "expert" automatically means you don't know very much about anything else.

So those looking for 30 min of fame can easily become public "experts" about things they really don't know much about. Possibly egged on by the university external relations team, these new-found media-friendly experts become a phone call away for well-meaning journalists who might not know whether that person is best to refer to about a particular matter.

On the other hand, a principled academic will be very coy when asked to comment publicly about things in which they are not expert.

Often-obscure academic research activities need to be funded, so the experts will apply for grant money through contestable funding rounds. These will come from either small pots of money within the university, or larger pots which are usually backed by the government. The Marsden Fund, administered by the Royal Society of NZ is a good example of the latter.

Sometimes academics can get money directly from the Govt if their expertise is topical or their esoteric area suddenly becomes important. For example, if we got signs that one of our big volcanoes was becoming active then the expert volcanologists would be flavour of the month, getting media time and possibly government contracts.

During the COVID pandemic it's been the 'modelers' and the epidemiologists who are the experts du jour. But that doesn't mean they will know anything about the psychological, societal, or financial impact of a lockdown. Other people are better qualified to talk about that.

Nevertheless, there's nothing stopping our original "experts" writing an Opinion Piece for the newspaper, but then they would have to decide whether to use the term 'opinionist' next to their name rather than 'scientist'.

Being an academic in NZ is a tough gig. I'm glad I'm not (literally) shedding blood, sweat, and tears in the exercise physiology lab anymore, although I do miss interacting with enthusiastic students. But I'm not banging my head against the door of the 'old-boys club' funding game nor having to add a cultural spin on everything.

The best bit though, is that it allows me to be a passionate opinionist!

Herd Mentality

"Regrets, I've had a few...", sang Frank Sinatra, but mostly he did things his way.

I tend to think you can't regret past decisions because you weigh up the pros and cons at the time and decide based on those. Occasionally though, some outside influence plays a part, and that's where decision-making goes pear-shaped.

Something I really regret is not standing up for someone when I was a teenager.

This kid, who occasionally caught the school bus, had a cleft palate. Most of the other kids politely didn't stare. Except one loud mouthed back-seat bully who, one day, told him very loudly that he was ugly.

That cruel remark would have been cutting and with long-lasting effects. I remember feeling deep compassion for the cleft palate kid and thinking that the bully was just that. But I did nothing, even though I could have sorted the bully-boy out.

You see, none of the other kids did anything, and I was too cool, scared, or whatever, to not go with the group decision. I did nothing because I didn't want to stand out or be different by sticking up for the kid who really needed help at that moment.

The cleft palate kid never caught the bus again, and I have not forgotten.

Most people don't want to stand out. They want to be part of the crowd, the herd if you must. So, for the vast majority, doing something or not doing something, is much easier if everyone else is doing that too. Even if sometimes it's not the right thing.

According to Wikipedia, 'herd', 'pack', or 'mob' mentality, "... describes how people can be influenced by their peers to adopt certain behaviours on a largely emotional, rather than rational, basis". When influenced by mob mentality, you are likely to make a different decision than you would if you were on your Pat.

Dedicated followers of fashion are sucked into the herd. Fashion is an obvious example of herd mentality in action.

Governments employ it, some for good and some for evil.

For example, the vaccination campaign has employed peer pressure through herd mentality to get people vaccinated. Our government calls it a 'team' approach for the greater good.

On the other hand, discrimination and even atrocities on certain populations in war time are assigned to a herd-mentality propagated by a ruling party. The 'Yellow Peril' xenophobic campaigns of the last century are just one illustration of this.

Herd mentality is a tool people should allow their government to use very carefully lest the rulers get a taste for it.

A herd mentality exists in academia too, even though 'The Academy' should be a bastion of individual thinking and free speech.

A case in point was the unsavoury way a mob of academics recently piled onto seven of their senior peers in response to a letter in the "Listener" magazine regarding proposed changes to the school curriculum.

The proposed changes give parity to Mātauranga Māori with the traditional sciences. More specifically, they also encourage the narrative that "science has been used to support the dominance of Eurocentric views, and the notion that science is a Western European invention and itself evidence of European dominance over Māori and other indigenous peoples."

The seven senior academics said that although indigenous knowledge may play a role in the preservation of local practice and in management and policy, it "falls far short of what can be defined as science itself". They say Mātauranga Māori should not be accepted as an equivalent to science, adding "it may help ... but it is not science".

The mob went into over-drive, Auckland University distancing itself from its own senior staff, and a petition set up Professors Siouxsie Wiles and Shaun Hendy to admonish and refute their colleagues. The Royal Society of NZ jumped on the bandwagon, ordering an investigation into the behaviour of the seven. The Tertiary Education Union also weighed in, like the Royal Society, seemingly unaware of the enormous contribution that non-European (Arabic, Asian, and American) people have made to science over the last thousand years.

But it's more than a little worrying when our Royal Society, a tax-payer funded organization set up by Act of Parliament and responsible for "the promotion of public awareness, knowledge, and understanding of science, technology, and the humanities…" is more influenced by mob mentality than its own constitution. I suspect it might already be regretting its decision to "investigate".

Someone standing up to a mob, disagreeing, saying something unfashionable, or looking at something from a different angle is when science and indeed academia is at its most productive. But it takes courage and a thick skin.

In the instantaneous world of social media, a mob or herd mentality can develop before anyone can spend enough time to properly consider an issue.

And like the bully shouting down the aisle from the back of the bus, Hendy, Wiles et al. used the distance of social media to create a mob when they could have just walked over to their colleagues' building and had an adult chat in the departmental tearoom.

If I did not write this Opinion Piece I would regret it.

The Big Experiment

One thing I don't miss about being an academic is the ordeal of getting research published.

Once you have a data set from an experiment, you write up the study and then send the manuscript away to a journal for publication. Before it's accepted for publication it must pass the rigors of 'peer-review' - critique from experts who look to find fault in your data collection or interpretation of the data. If the reviewers find serious flaws, such as in the study design, it's rejected and unable to be published. If they find only minor issues, they give you the chance to amend the manuscript, then it can be published.

Creating new knowledge through research is useless unless it's published somewhere so that other people can read it and learn from it, so getting a study published is vital.

One study we did in my role as a Professor of Sport Physiology, involved supplying bikes to a local primary school to measure the effect of school-time riding on the physical fitness of the children. We assumed (hypothesized) that cycling would improve fitness, so we measured this in the children before and after we gave them the bikes for two terms.

At the completion of the study we were pleased to see, as hypothesized, small but positive changes in fitness between term 2 and term 4. So, we wrote the study up and sent it away to a journal for publication.

That's where things became messy. The reviewers said, "How can you be sure that supplying your bikes (the 'intervention') was the cause of the improvement in fitness?". Perhaps, they said, it was that it was getting warmer in spring, or that the kids were growing, and that's why their fitness improved. Unlikely, but they had a point.

When we'd designed the study, we did not have a 'control' (comparison) group. That is, we did not also measure the fitness of a group of children at the school of the same age who did not have access to the bikes; kids who were not given the 'intervention'. If we did have a control group, and their fitness also improved over two terms, then clearly something aside from providing the bicycles was behind improved fitness in our intervention group. If fitness of the control group didn't improve, then our hypothesis (that supplying bikes improves fitness) would be correct.

So, after all that work we could not get the study published because we had a major flaw in the study design as we weren't actually able to confidently test our hypothesis.

The problem was that ethically we could not have given some kids bikes and others not. In NZ, that sort of thing is deemed not fair (not ethical) because it is generally assumed to be advantageous to children to have the opportunity to ride.

So we are never going to be 100% sure that supplying bikes to a school helps the students' fitness, and we can't tell anyone else what we'd done through a publication.

And so it is with NZ's biggest ever social experiment. After the pandemic has subsided, we are never going to know whether our intervention (the 'lock-down') was useful in saving lives. This is because we don't have a control group of Kiwis who were not locked down.

Although we could actually do this – we are ideally placed with a large spare island to the south – it would not be ethical because the experts assume there is some advantage to being locked down.

Because places such as Sweden and the Netherlands, with somewhat similar populations, have chosen for a much lighter version of a lockdown, we could try to make some comparisons with those countries. But the seasons are different, the lifestyles different, and the genetic and cultural nature of their people are quite different to ours, so considering these as 'controls' would be flawed.

So we must trust in the untested hypotheses of experts, the likes of Drs Baker and Bloomfield, and collectively do what they assume is best for our population.

But when it's all said and done, they will struggle to get this big experiment published.

Why do we ask "Why?"

I vaguely remember as a child asking my father questions about many and varied things, because I was sure he was the fountain of all knowledge. That was well before the middle teenage years at which point I suddenly knew much more than him.

Many years later, I recall my children asking me about things; "Why is grass green?", "Why isn't there a king?", "Why can't I spend my Monopoly money at Pak-N-Save?". Being able to confidently answer these makes you feel useful and important as a parent, and as such, questions were encouraged. There was certainly no penalty for questioning things.

In the small world of my wife's mothers' group, one youngster was rather too regularly asking "Why?". Mum finally asked the young fellow in exasperation, "You ask a lot of questions, don't you Callum?". To which the six-year-old replied, "Yes mummy, but why?".

We could take a leaf out of Callum's book and take the opportunity to ask why more often. Perhaps not the bleeding obvious like why we can't trade Marylebone Station for a frozen chook at the supermarket, but thinking about what we, us and them, often do and why we do it.

We should review why do we do things personally, and as a culture. Longstanding things and things more recent. And the start of that process is asking "Why?".

Why don't we eat meat and three veg for breakfast?

Why is milk white?

Why do we drive up and down the carpark looking for the spot closest to the shop when the empty spot in the corner is only a 45 second walk?

Why do we complain about our politicians?

Why do we have front lawns?

Why do people wear a mask when driving the car alone?

Why don't we have medals for fourth?

Sometimes the answer is obvious and sensible, sometimes it's historical. Sometimes there isn't a good answer, including, "It's what we did last year".

Anyway, sometimes when you ask why, you're the only one that has the guts to do so, and everyone else wants to know the answer!

If I ask a question about something it doesn't mean I don't agree with it. It's just that I want to know how and why. Like Callum. Then if I know how and why I can think about it and make my mind up.

But in modern NZ there is the assumption that if you question something you are automatically against it.

Perhaps that comes from our political debates where the opposing parties or reporters ask questions in a blatant attempt to trap or discredit others for what they are doing.

It also seems to have become more prevalent in academia, where rather than reasoned arguments parleyed with intellect and wit, one side responds to questions with dismissal or derision.

Regardless, the general assumption these days is that if you are questioning something you are against it.

The result is that too many hui conclude without the hard questions being asked - Kiwi's don't like to stand out by putting their head above the parapet and they will especially avoid confronting or awkward situations. But hey, once the meeting concludes, the whingeing starts afresh.

If asked what my biggest concern about the current state of affairs is in NZ, my answer isn't the looming recession or inflation. Not Three Waters or co-governance. It would be how easily those with the intestinal fortitude to ask the hard questions are shut down because they are automatically seen as being obverse.

Rarely does someone reply gently with an educational tone or point of view. Rather, the first port of call seems to be ridicule, rank-pulling or some level of personal attack.

Questions about things that affect us all should be welcomed, even if they might seem dumb, stupid, or even politically motivated. And if the questions do happen to be loaded or mischievous, then they should be easily parried.

Nevertheless, like young Callum, there should be no penalty for just asking.

The sixth sense of AI

Some people I know have a sixth sense.

Sometimes that extra sense presents as being intuitive about a person or situation, other times it might be described as possessing a good 'bull-shit' meter.

Others I know have a sense that can "read" a sports game well. They are top football/rugby/hockey players and able to sense what might happen in a moment's time and that prediction helps them beat the opposition.

And I've met people who reckon they can sense the goodness (or otherwise) in people through their eyes.

Animals can sense things we can't. For example, many animals know when earthquakes are coming well before we humans do. Our backyard chickens have a sixth sense; they only have to see my wife to know they are in trouble. Granted that might be more to do with the voodoo chicken she repeatedly skewers when they dig up her flowering bulbs.

Artificial intelligence (AI) is the next big thing. If predictions come true, it will enable us to cure cancer, send robots to nearby planets, and pass the end of year exams without studying. Predictions also include massive job replacement, from aged care workers to radiologists.

Like anything artificial though, you only get out what you put in.

Examples of AI already in use include search engine optimization, facial recognition, self-driving cars, Google Map directions, reconnaissance drones, personalised ads, and the detection of fraudulent banking transactions.

One example in use in NZ for some years is vehicle number plate recognition. It's used on toll ways to identify a vehicle and instantly charge accordingly. Increasingly it is used in parking stations to meter length of stay. The process is set to automatically send fines out if a car is there too long.

My wife got a fine the other day for parking in a supermarket carpark for eight hours. Now neither of us likes shopping that much that we'd park in at a supermarket for eight hours. Certainly not on the day in question because it was a busy day for both of us in our café.

However, on that day between us we went to that supermarket three times, in the same car, to pick up supplies for the café.

Quite clearly, the AI - we'll call it HAL - either did not recognise that our car left the carpark each time except the last, or chose not to. HAL simply took the first entry and the last exit, and hey presto, a $60 fine.

Perhaps HAL is mistakenly programmed like that? Or maybe it/they has a low Artificial IQ. It certainly could not conceive that a car might come and go from the same carpark a number of times during the day.

We have managed to sort it out without having to reason with a bot on the phone. Bots from NZ don't understand Australian accents for a start. It took the intervention of a real person.

The above is an example where AI can't process things outside of its expectations; the parameters which have been put in by humans.

I gather there are types of machine-learning that improve the performance of an AI process, and other situations where humans can update the parameters, avoiding on-going situations like those described above.

Meanwhile though, I suspect there are increasing numbers of people getting wrongly caught, like my wife, by HAL and his ilk, and then having to deal with the fall out.

In any automated process such as the parking AI described above, there needs to be a human involved somewhere along the line so reasoning can take place if necessary. That human needs to understand the weaknesses of that particular process and bypass the AI where necessary. It's going to be a scary world when this doesn't happen and you have to reason with a bot.

Further still, AI certainly won't have the intuition a person can possess; a working bull-shit meter or that sixth sense.

AI will never be a good judge of a person, be able to look into their eyes and determine if they are trustworthy or look at an opponent and know where they are going to pass the ball.

Call me a Luddite, but we'd be best to ship our NZ bots and AI off to Australia and raise the Artificial IQ in both countries.

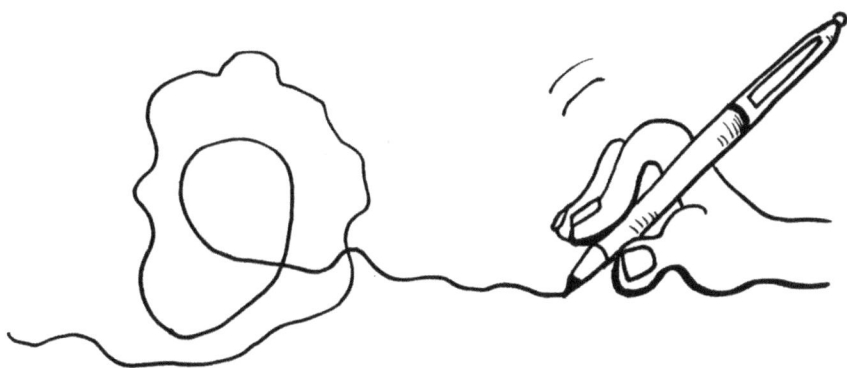

Education

Learning something new from something old

Women on Top

How to use a longer lever to get your wheel nuts off

Learning something new from something old

When undertaking laboratory experiments it is wise to employ protocols or methods which have been previously published by other scientists because it means that the methodology is deemed acceptable to your peers. Even better if it's a protocol which has been described many times in a textbook because there will be little argument about its validity and reliability.

One method, often used in fitness testing on the treadmill, is the 'Bruce' protocol. It describes the way the treadmill increases in speed and incline as the test gets harder for the person on the treadmill. The idea being that it will get so fast and steep that they will reach a point of exhaustion and will stop. When heart rate and other physiological data are simultaneously collected and aligned with the time point of cessation, it tells you something about the cardio-respiratory fitness and thus state of health of the person being tested.

The Bruce protocol is used regularly when investigating the fitness of non-athletes, including overweight people and people with suspected cardiovascular disease.

One issue which seemed to arise for me when using the 'Bruce' was that the incline of the treadmill became quite steep at about the point of transition from a run to a walk. This made it very awkward for many study participants and I often felt that they would fatigue prematurely because of this. But, since it was a "textbook" protocol, I assumed many minds wiser than mine had put much thought into the design.

The late Peter Snell, whom I counted as a friend and learned exercise physiology colleague, was visiting us in Wellington some years ago whilst we were in the midst of a study. We were using the Bruce protocol and, as usual, the study participants struggled at that critical point of gait transition.

When explaining to him what we were doing, he said in his straight-to-the-point fashion, "What are you using that protocol for?"

"We wanted to use something textbook, something that when reviewed by peers, would be deemed best practice" was, from memory, my guarded reply.

Then Peter explained that the Bruce protocol was invented by an American cardiologist named, not surprisingly, Robert Bruce. A paper describing his methods was published in the journal 'Pediatrics' in 1963 and has been cited ever since. Peter went on to explain that the reason Dr Bruce chose the particular speed/incline protocol was because it was the only gearing speed and incline ratios which his old treadmill could manage! So, there was certainly no complex thinking behind the famous Bruce protocol. Sir Peter knew this because his job for many years at the University of Texas Southwestern, meant liaising with the US medical crowd, and Dr Bruce was one of them.

Anyhow, at that point I felt like an ill-informed novice, but it taught me a couple of lessons.

Firstly, having some experienced grey headed people around you as you go about your business is a good thing, as you might just learn something new from something old.

Secondly, even though something is considered a fact or well accepted, it doesn't hurt to go back and look at why/how it was developed or discovered and then make your own mind up about it.

Lastly, how some small piece of knowledge can become inflated or cemented as textbook-knowledge even when the background story is spurious. And this is usually because the vast majority of people are too lazy or not confident enough to question the status quo.

I'm sure there are plenty of "facts" in many academic disciplines that have slipped through the net of periodic scrutiny and are now cemented as dogma or doctrine. One has to be particularly careful of these when sharing knowledge with the next generation; in a school curriculum for instance.

Currently there is debate as to what knowledge is considered "scientific" in origin. Without partaking in that argument, I can say that good science should always be allowed to question and test what's written in a textbook or what's currently accepted as common knowledge. Because you never know just what you might learn.

Women on Top

There's a page which pops up on my Facebook feed entitled 'Why women live longer than men'. It's essentially a collection of photos showing men creating absurdly dangerous contraptions or set-ups to get a job done.

Reaching the chimney by strapping two ladders end-to-end; getting to the factory ceiling by putting your scissor-lift atop an extended fork-lift; feeding the alligators by hand or such like. It's a theme of innovation and stupidity which, while creative, has a high chance of leading to death or destruction of man and machine. Some perhaps would suggest "the good ole days" on the building site, but Work Safe would suggest litigation. The majority of these pictures are from developing countries where smart-phone cameras are common, but common sense is not.

In NZ men are more likely to be killed in workplace accidents than women, maybe because they are more likely to work dangerous jobs, maybe because they are stupid, or perhaps because they are more likely to take a chance.

Not following the flock, men will do something alone, against the grain, outside the box, something risky. I'm generalizing terribly of course, but so do epidemiologists.

On the other hand, risk aversion is why women prefer team sports, spend recreational and social occasions in groups, and put their savings in term deposits rather than shares. But it also means they often "pick up the pieces" men create.

However, greater risk goes with greater reward, particularly in business. Maybe it's why men are more likely to climb to the top but also become bankrupt.

To counter the excess of men in high places, women-only initiatives pop up all over NZ - Women in Business, Women in Leadership, Women in Science, even a Ministry for Women.

I can only surmise the agendas for these collectives but sensibly they must, at least sometimes, discuss men and the way they operate in the workplace. Maybe they show pictures from, 'Why women live longer...'? If you don't discuss why men behave differently, why have a women-only group?

There's nothing wrong with single sex groups or activities, and certainly there's nothing wrong with learning how the other sex operates. Except that these days if you had a men's-only group of anything apart from model railways, you'd be taken to court.

Perhaps though the assumed necessity for having women's only groups would subside if the issue of gender inequality in the NZ education system was addressed.

In 2019 in NZ, only one sixth of Primary School teachers were male. At High School the inequality is less marked where 38% of teaching staff are male, and at polytechs and university the gender mix is about equal, though with more younger women academics off-setting the slightly higher number of over 65 males. Wananga students are taught predominantly by women.

In these days of equality, I'm miffed as to why there's no national strategy to train and employ men as teachers in the formative Primary School years. Like the stated government's commitment to increase women's participation to 50 percent on state sector boards and committees.

Equality of gender representation at the boardroom level is said to improve business practice, better use human capital, and provide role models for women. Along the same lines, having more male primary school teachers would surely provide more positive male role models and attenuate the declining educational performance of boys.

The situation is worse at single-sex high schools. While there are less women than men teaching at boys-only high schools, male teachers at girls-only schools are as rare as rocking horse poo.

If we really wanted our young women to better understand how men operate in the workplace, we could start by addressing the issue of why more men don't teach at Primary School and especially at girls-only high schools.

How to use a longer lever to get your wheel nuts off

It is no secret that NZ school students are falling further behind in maths and science knowledge compared with other countries.

The Trends in International Mathematics and Science Study (TIMSS) is performed once every four years. It focuses on assessing student achievement in maths and science at middle primary (NZ Year 5) and lower secondary (NZ Year 9) levels around the world. While it's coordinated in the US, here it's managed by our Ministry of Education. Our Year 9 students maths ability now ranks 23rd out of 39 countries and in science, 17th from 35. Fair to middling in comparison, but these are decreases from the previous surveys in 2014, and notably worse than fifteen years ago.

While our own 'Einsteins' (outliers) will still pop up occasionally, and become tomorrow's McDiarmids and Callaghans, it means the general ability of the average NZ young person to think like a scientist, or solve a maths-based problem themselves, is declining. And there will be outliers in the direction of Homer Simpson as well.

Maybe if a youngster has his or her heart set on being a manicurist or rugby player, maths and science ability is not especially useful. But at least a rudimentary understanding of maths is pretty useful for budgeting or building a deck.

I have three degrees, all science-based. The first being a Bachelor of Science in Agriculture, which provided a terrific grounding in much of the physical sciences (physics, chemistry, maths) as well as life-sciences (physiology, biology, botany etc.).

My latter postgraduate education was in human nutrition and physiology, but there I often relied on my basic physical science knowledge to help understand the esoteric nature of what I was trying to get my head around.

The biggest impact this science knowledge has meant to me is that I now act like a scientist as I live my life as an environmentally aware citizen and small business owner. Making sure the doors are closed in winter to keep the cold air out, driving carefully to reduce fuel use and save money, modelling sales from previous years to see when it's best to take a holiday. Even wearing jandals and socks at home in winter to stop my body heat dissipating into the cold kitchen floor.

Being a scientist is more than actions, it's also a way of thinking. My science career taught me to ask if something can be done better, or whether there is an alternative explanation for some observation. It means challenging dogma, asking the questions, entering a debate armed with some data, or questioning "the narrative". These can make you unpopular, especially in NZ.

Being a scientist is NOT about assuming someone is right without taking the time to form an evidence-based opinion. No one, after all, has won a Nobel prize in medicine/physiology for re-hashing knowledge from a textbook.

And scientists don't resort to name-calling someone who disagrees with them on the current and popular explanation. Good science enables and encourages robust debate, but wins the debate with weight of empirical evidence.

My worry is that the next generation, whose grasp of science and mathematics is less than the previous, won't be able to think in a scientific way on a day to day basis. They won't understand the importance of simple things like enabling airflow to keep a house dry, using a longer lever to get your wheel nuts off, or exercising to keep warm. They won't draw a conclusion and win an argument based on evidence, but rather rely on weight of media exposure.

And when scientifically naïve people are in charge and make decisions based solely on popularity and emotion, we will be in trouble.

Perhaps we should not be surprised that all sorts of quirky and popular theories and conspiracies are now so easily accepted by so many. They are probably lacking a good school science education.

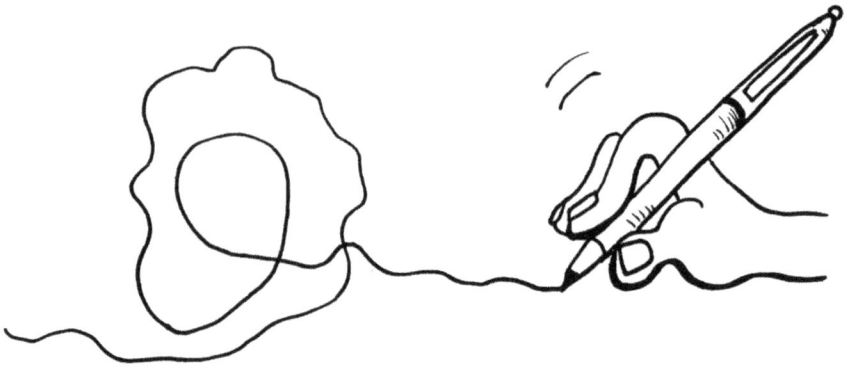

Politics and Bureaucracy

Why Palmy would make a better NZ capital city than Wellington

A futile cycle

You should only be elected if you've wiped someone else's bottom

An insidious bank fee that retailers pay

How to get the bank and the government to pay your mortgage

Throwing the first punch

The Road Cone Epidemic

Why Palmy would make a better NZ capital city than Wellington

Wellington is in disarray. Their water supply is as leaky as a cabinet meeting. Their roads are narrow and windy, and not suitable for public transport. Much of the housing stock sits tenuously on the side of slippery hills, and the whole place sits on an active fault line.

There are only two roads out of the place, and one can be easily closed with snow or a minor traffic accident. The airport is just about as dubious as the weather and can't take anything bigger than a small passenger jet. On most days it takes longer to get from the central city to the airport than it does to fly to Dunedin.

If you had a blank canvas and you wanted to choose a city somewhere to house your seat of government, you absolutely positively would not choose Wellington.

According to its City Council website, Wellington became New Zealand's capital in 1865. The decision to house our parliament there was made by a panel of Australian-based commissioners "... due to its favourable geography, sheltered harbour and central location".

They'd obviously never been to Wellington.

The politicians and bureaucrats down there don't get out much. They are stuck in their offices and coffee shops because of the angry weather and difficulty in leaving the place. Consequently, they are completely out of touch with the rest of the country.

They are getting us to change the way we manage our water, but can't manage their own. They want the rest of the country to improve their traffic management, but they can't sort out their own. And proofing buildings for future earthquakes, for them, just requires increasing taxes and rates when for many small towns, the same requirements will send businesses and residents broke.

Politicians need to be able to easily get out of their offices so that they are not out of touch. They need to mix with people representative of all of NZ, not just fellow politicians and those paid solely by the tax-take.

They need to be able to fill their own car, ride a bicycle on a narrow road while being passed by a milk tanker, go to the recently robbed corner store, and cop an earful from the local council worker who's sick of filling in potholes.

Nearly a decade ago there was some discussion about de-centralising government departments just in case there was a really big shake in Wellington. Back then the impact of Christchurch was still raw.

In this very masthead in 2017 Palmerston North Mayor Grant Smith suggested that if functions should be decentralised, and "Palmerston North, was well-placed to take over defence". That sounds sensible to me. The only tank I've seen in Wellington is one leaking water.

Some recent news articles have attempted to gee up the downcast Wellingtonians, who in a moment of self-reflection, have finally realized what a shambles the infrastructure there is in.

I learnt from my sporting competition days, that if your opponent is struggling, that's the time to "put the boot in".

Well, Wellington is struggling at the moment and so I reckon it's time Palmy stole the Capital moniker from them.

It'd be an offer too good to refuse. They get rid of the politicians, and we'd get 'Let's Get Palmy Moving'. Because as one of my customers pointed out to me recently, we have two Tony's Tyre Services whereas Wellington only has one.

Now don't get me wrong; I like Wellington. Thrice a year, when they are endowed with a beautiful clear windless day, it's the best city on the North Island south of Levin. And I have to admit, the coffee in Wellington is nearly as good as Palmerston North. Oh, and the museum down there, Te Papa, is worth a visit too.

From Palmerston North you can get out of town any direction you want, and in terms of defense, our region is only missing the Navy. With our windmills, the Rugby Museum, and free parking on Sundays, Palmy is clearly the superior place to locate NZ Parliament.

Anyway, we already have the Capital Connection and a whole precinct across the river with plenty of empty rooms.

54

You'd know they really want to be the people's representatives if politicians had to live here. And they'd get way better bang for their $52K accommodation supplement buck here than they would in Wellington.

Goodness, I'd even take in a politician as a boarder if they were to pay me that much. Probably a Green one because I've got plenty of bicycles I can lend them.

A futile cycle

In biochemistry there is a term called 'futile cycling' that describes a series of chemical reactions which take place to no net gain but a loss of energy. For example, in our body fat cells (adipocytes) large fat molecules called triglycerides are constantly being broken down to their smaller constituent parts (fatty acids and glycerol) and then put back together. Each time this happens some energy leaks out (as heat) and we end up where we started but with a little less energy available to use for useful things like muscle contraction.

Those who fondly recall their high school chemistry classes will recognize that this energy cost is an example of 'entropy' increasing – described by the 2nd Law of Thermodynamics; an energy cost for no obvious gain.

It's like playing Monopoly, but instead of getting $200 when you land on 'GO', it costs you $200 before you are allowed to do the next lap of the board.

Doing business in NZ is like that. There is a plethora of costs you incur or hoops you must jump through before you can trade, most related to compliance of some law or regulation. A food/building/backflow inspection here, a waste water levy there, ACC and council rates everywhere. All have to be paid before you can open the door to let a customer in, before you can make any money, before you can pay your staff, before you can pay any tax to support the country and pay our politicians.

And where do all those levies and taxes go? Primarily to pay the wages of those people employed to do the inspections or monitor compliance! It's a futile cycle that absorbs money but seemingly for no apparent gain.

There is often an historical and sensible reason for many of these, especially around safety of customers and staff. No restaurant owner wants to poison their customers with green ham and eggs, so occasional food inspections are there to keep you on your food safety (fully covered) toes. And having an unobstructed fire escape at the match factory may come in handy for the product testing staff at some point.

In New Zealand, more so than elsewhere, we are faced with the "safety fads" that come around every so often. Earthquake strengthening, which seems reasonable immediately after (or before!) an earthquake, is essentially useless for the next 100 years. Then there is asbestos inspection, and I hear that the next big thing coming is a mandatory business pandemic plan. All of these are created in the hope of possibly preventing injury or worse to someone, but they do come at significant cost to a business.

However, the reasons for some of the "hoops" are ridiculous. When John Doe from Small Widget in 1978 had a deadlock on the front door of his shop, the poor arsonist couldn't get out after he lit the petrol can because he couldn't find the key to the deadbolt. So now you'll only pass the building inspection – which you pay for thanks very much – if you can't deadlock your premises after hours. Because in NZ we pride ourselves on keeping our arsonists and burglars safe.

Or if the mirror in the disabled bathroom is 3 cm too high you won't pass the inspection, i.e. you can't trade unless you move it down low enough so a person in a wheel chair can see their lips. Fair enough. But on the other hand, you pass the inspection if you don't have a mirror at all, in which case the wheelchair bound customer can't even see their hair let alone their lipstick.

Biochemists suggest that our cells evolved futile cycling because it helps maintain a basal level of biochemical 'machinery' which can be cranked up quickly just in case the need arises, like running away from a sabre-toothed tiger. Similarly, a good portion of our by-laws and rules that are there just in case that one in a million happens - like seeing that sabre-toothed tiger in the bathroom mirror.

It's no wonder that NZ workers do some of the longest hours in the world but get told their productivity is poor. You can be certain that pretty soon some career politician will tell us that businesses need to work more efficiently, or smarter, so we can generate the money to pay for pandemics like COVID. But you can also be sure that the same law-maker will add another hoop for business, or a new tax or levy, in political response to a 'squeaky wheel' or a one-in-a-hundred year event.

If the do-gooders in Parliament could also work smarter by removing some of the futile cycling we might be able to harness that energy for business activity, generate some tax, and finally get to pass Go.

You should only be elected if
you've wiped someone else's bottom

It's been disappointing that COVID has permeated politics, one side blaming the other for things that are often beyond control. I reckon pretty much everyone is trying their best, especially those on the ground at the border.

With election time coming up, I've started to think about who I might vote for. It won't be for anyone whose primary strategy is to critically bleat on about what's happening without coming up with a viable plan.

I want a person elected who comprehends the community, the people in it, what they do, and what their worries are. Someone who knows more than just political spin, someone who has had life experience. Someone with empathy, and genuine interest in the lives of others. It's a huge responsibility being a politician, and it takes a special person with a thick skin.

My mum, a special person and now elderly, was a trained physiotherapist who spent much of her working life aiding disabled people and those in nursing homes. Working with her clientele must have been difficult, as so many of them had little potential for functional improvement, although maintenance might have been the goal much of the time.

In hindsight I think that, especially for those in nursing homes, just the visit from her was something they would look forward to. Some social interaction and some physical touch from another human, many of whom would have no-one to visit on a regular basis.

As children, my four sisters and I all played some sort of musical instrument, all of my sisters more accomplished than I. But each Christmas my mother would take us around to the nursing homes and we'd give a small group of residents a little concert.

We used to hate it because, as kids, the last thing you want to do is be surrounded by a bunch of old or strange people in a funny smelling place when you could be down at the park playing cricket. But I recall most of the residents enjoyed our little show because there were plenty of smiles and the odd sing-a-long. Some of the enjoyment was probably because it was something different, brightening an afternoon when for most it was "ground hog day" until they died. I do remember one elderly gent who told me that he also played the clarinet in his youth and loudly noted to the rest of the room that "I used to be much better than that"!

Doing a few years of these Christmas concert "seasons" gave my sisters and I a level of comfort dealing with old people and disabled people. It certainly gave me a respect and sense of value for these people, all of whom were contributors to society in some way, and many of whom held gems of information or stories which I'd have loved to have tapped into.

As young adults my sisters and I subsequently did some sort of paid or voluntary work with disabled or elderly people. Sometimes that meant feeding them, literally hand to mouth, and assisting them to walk or move. Sometimes it meant taking them to the toilet and cleaning up afterwards.

These were life experiences, growing up times for me, and I'm glad I had them because it showed me part of a world outside my own. I'm disappointed my kids haven't had those same opportunities to date, but I guess they've had different ones. Lock-downs in their part of the world for example. And who knows, in the future they might have to wipe the snot from my nose or change my nappy, much like I did for them. Only time and David Seymour's referendum will tell.

So, I've decided that you should only be elected if you've wiped someone else's bottom.

An insidious bank fee that retailers pay

Most people who come into my café to buy a coffee use a card for payment. I'd reckon less than 10% of customers use cash these days.

Payment by card is easy because the staff don't have to handle cash, including the calculations involved, and there is an immediate money trail.

It's easy for the customer too, because they don't have to worry about holding cash, and they can pay with just a 'wave' of their card, phone, or smart watch.

But that service the banks provide costs money. The median cost is around 2% of a transaction value. Using a debit card costs very little, but using an international credit card costs nearly 5% of the money taken.

At our little café at the moment, and indeed at big retailers like supermarkets, the cost of that card service is not added to the customer's bill. The business just absorbs the cost because it's more trouble to collect it.

Ten cents added to a $5 cup of coffee is hardly noticeable to the drinker. But for a retailer whose margin might be only $2.50 per cup, this becomes a 4% levy. Over the space of a year this can add up to thousands of dollars for a small business like mine.

The bank is providing a service to me and to the customer, so I've been happy to pay it. For now at least.

But many smaller businesses and probably my own if I could work out how to do it, are now passing on that cost to the customer.

However, if you dig a bit deeper you will find that it's another situation where it's 1:nil in the battle of the Banks vs the Public.

Let's say you go to the dress shop and spend $100 and use your credit card. The dress shop owner's bank account will receive $100, on "paper" but $13.04 of that is put aside to pay GST. At the moment the card was used, the bank took $2 for card fees.

However, and this is the critical point, the dress shop has paid GST on $100, not $100 minus GST, the amount the shop owner actually gets. In other words, the dress shop owner is paying a bank charge for collecting the GST on behalf of IRD.

The dress shop owner is then left with $84.96 she can spend after GST and bank charges are accounted for.

The dress shop owner goes to the independent hardware store next door and spends that $84.96 buying a new portable heater for her shop so she can keep warm. By the time the GST and card charges are accounted for, there is $72.18 that the hardware store can spend. But again, the hardware store is paying GST on $84.96, not the actual amount the hardware shop earns ($84.96 minus GST).

Extrapolating this, after 25 similar transactions on the same working day, from the original $100 there is only $1.70 left. Of the $98.30 which has disappeared into the financial 'ether', the government has collected $85.23 GST and the banks have collected $13.07 in card charges.

Firstly, you can see how good the concept of a GST is for tax collection. Admittedly, perhaps Inland Revenue gets only half that $85 because the businesses can claim a portion of that GST back. It's still a very good earner though.

Secondly, you can see how insidious the bank charges are, and therefore how profitable card use is for banks. Not surprisingly banks don't want us to use cash. In fact they discourage it by limiting cash deposits and geographically thinning out ATMs.

Lastly, IRD is asking retailers to pay bank charges on collecting GST on their behalf. My back of the envelope calculation suggests that for every $100 spent in the community the banks are over $1.50 better off because retailers are paying the bank charges on the GST-inclusive sale amount rather than the GST-exclusive amount.

Now work out how much money is spent in NZ on cards every day and take 1.5% of that. It's a massive amount of money that IRD is paying the banks to collect GST on their behalf.

The banks are laughing all the way to the bank!

When a GST was introduced here in the mid-eighties, there was a decision made not to charge GST on bank transactions because it would be too messy. I can see that. But banking has changed; card payment was rare when cricket players wore beige.

There are financial minds greater than mine who would argue for the current situation, though probably not small shop owners. And perhaps the banks will argue that they are doing a service on behalf of IRD.

Nonetheless, if you spend cash when you shop you are preventing the banks clipping the ticket through card use and arguably avoiding GST responsibilities.

No wonder they want to get rid of the folding stuff.

How to get the bank and the government to pay your mortgage

If you are self-employed you'll know how hard it is to get a loan from the bank.

I suppose the banks see a heightened risk involved in lending to a business owner, especially at the moment when many are having difficulty operating through a recession.

Banks dish out loans because it's a very good earner for them. But banks don't want those loans to go bad, especially if the money borrowed is not backed by assets which could be liquidated (sold) to cover any debt.

Lending money to a salary earner to buy a house is "as safe as houses" because if the person cannot meet their mortgage repayments and default, then the house can be sold and the debt recovered.

Lending to a business is more tricky, as debt can quickly accumulate as unpaid bills and unpaid tax, and you can't sell those to recover costs. In fact, it's the main reason why businesses pay their tax upfront – provisional tax. If they go belly-up, IRD has already been paid.

On the other hand, it's business activity and it is the tax taken from that which enables us to pay for government services, including activities like policing and a public health system. It also pays for the overheads associated with government services, like politicians.

For a business to prosper it needs to produce goods with a decent value-add; the difference between the value of goods put into a process and the value of what comes out. The higher that 'margin', the greater the tax take from that item, especially GST. So, when NZ business is producing valuable goods (or services), then our government has plenty of money to invest in things like new cancer drugs and the education system.

However, for a business to create more value from their ingredients they often need to invest in new equipment or processes. And that takes money. Farmers do this all the time, buying a new tractor for example, because the old one was too small, fuel inefficient, and less safe.

Unless a business has a decent cash surplus, the money for that new tractor needs to come from borrowing. But if the bank doesn't lend the money the tractor cannot be bought, the value-add on the farm outputs cannot increase, and the tax paid doesn't increase.

So, it was with surprise I read the article in the Manawatū Standard (15th May) about a young mum who managed to get a mortgage whilst on the Benefit.

Obviously, the mum is a careful spender, and in a previous situation had been able to save a deposit for her house through Kiwisaver.

She worked out that the income from the benefit she and her two kids were receiving was sufficient to service a small mortgage on a house in Dannevirke. The sums were done, the bank was convinced, and she now has a house and is independent, not needing to pay rent, or occupy social housing.

She really is what the newspaper article described her as "a Kiwi battler".

She was quoted as saying "that being on a benefit was not a barrier to getting a mortgage with her bank", as long as she "was able to prove to the bank her income was stable…"

My first thoughts when reading this, apart from admiration for the woman, was that there is no more "stable" an income than the benefit. It is underwritten by the taxpayer.

It's a win-win surely? Well, it is for the woman and the bank.

The story paints the bank who did the lending as benevolent, which is contrary to what we often hear about the behaviour of the banks.

But if you think about it a bit more, the actions of the bank perhaps aren't so altruistic. And the loser in this story is the taxpayer.

A mortgage of $156,600, which she has, paid weekly over 30 years at 7.25% (current rate at the time for six months fixed at the ANZ) requires interest payments of $227,735 over the life of the loan. So essentially, the bank is making $227,735 from the taxpayers of NZ who are paying the mortgage through the woman's benefit.

Now I don't have a beef with the woman who got the loan. All power to her for her determination and financial prudence.

But I do have a beef with the bank, who in this case is making money entirely off the tit of the taxpayer.

This woman's situation won't be a one-off. Anyone who is a net beneficiary and is also paying off a housing loan will have a mortgage which, to some extent, is paid for by the taxpayer.

Compare the woman's situation with a farmer. That farmer is generating GST, income tax, and employing others. Oh, and they are producing food as well.

Yet the farmer is paying 15.7% on their overdraft because the bank sees that lending as risky. And a farmer would need to jump through a hoop to get a separate loan for new plant and equipment, again at a much higher rate of interest than a mortgage holder.

Last week RNZ reported "Federated Farmers say intense banking pressure on farmers is taking a huge emotional toll - amid calls for an inquiry into the rural banking sector."

The first thing the inquiry needs to address is why the taxpayer is gifting money to profitable banks while farmers and other businesses who actually create value and produce tax, are penalized.

Throwing the first punch

As an academic exercise physiologist, I taught undergraduate (UG) skeletal muscle metabolism for many years. That topic revolved largely around how muscle used fuel that enabled it to contract.

Muscle contraction somewhere in the body is required for just about everything we do, but especially during exercise. So skeletal muscle metabolism is a pretty important topic!

For convenience and simplicity of understanding, we'd divide muscle metabolism into three parts according to the main fuel and then how long that fuel could sustain a contracting muscle.

When a muscle is asked, by the brain, to contract very forcefully and quickly, it uses and then exhausts its very short-term store of energy called creatine phosphate. You can get about 10 seconds, give or take, from that, going flat out.

From then on, if you try to keep going you need to transition to the next fuel, and that's called muscle glycogen, a form of carbohydrate stored inside your muscle. You won't be able to go quite as hard at that point but it'll keep you going for a good few minutes until other fuels like fat and carbohydrate from the blood can be taken up by the muscle and used.

McArdle Disease is a very rare genetic condition that does not let the sufferer utilize muscle glycogen. So, these people can get through that first ten seconds of exercise, then they crawl to a stop for ten minutes or so before they can get going again in (only) moderate exercise mode.

On one visit to Peter Snell in Dallas, when he was still working as an exercise physiologist, I was invited to a specialist lab there which diagnosed and tested those with McArdle.

A woman I met played softball as a youngster and couldn't work out why, when batting and she made a decent hit, she'd get past first base, but simply couldn't make second. She had McArdle disease.

Another fellow was a young line-backer who just could not make a touchdown. Needless to say his football career probably stalled as quickly as his running.

The same fellow noted that if he started a fight he'd have to finish it within ten seconds or he was in big trouble. He'd have to throw the first punches, and hard. No "fight or flight" options for him!

You'd have to have a really good reason to throw the first punch, and realistically, this fellow didn't really have a choice.

I was thinking about this fellow the other day in relation to recent happenings here in NZ where protests have turned violent.

Some protagonists involved in these protests seem to prepare for violence, talking about getting on the "front line". Others gate-crash what start as peaceful gatherings with collections of projectiles and stuff to hit others with.

In the vast majority of standoffs both parties do have a choice. If someone strikes first, they are the aggressor. It's not the done thing to take an argument from verbal aggression to physical aggression. We like to think in modern civilized society like Aotearoa that doesn't happen.

Best case is when nothing physical actually happens despite much bluster and bravado. Arm waving and spear rattling sans physical violence is how humans have survived for millions of years after all!

But I sense that here in NZ at the moment some groups think it acceptable to be the aggressor.

We are lucky in NZ that we are permitted to stay on first base. That is, we can "rattle our spears", puff up our chests, and protest sensibly, all with little consequence. Even when the opposition hasn't turned up!

But it's not acceptable, to "throw the spear" or the first punch. Such people need to be dealt by authorities accordingly, and I'm fairly confident here in NZ they will be.

The Road Cone Epidemic

The term asexual reproduction describes when an organism is able to reproduce on its own, where offspring are exactly the same as the parent because there is no other genetic input. It is the primary form of reproduction for single-celled organisms such as archaea and bacteria, and more recently, road cones.

In the dead of night, when no one is looking, usually in the summer, road cones are able to breed, and by morning they have exploded in number.

They line the road or path to produce avenues of fluoro-orange, spilling over into driveways and footpaths, especially around holes and newly laid gravel. Often they are seen paired with a speed sign, as if in symbiosis, but mostly they are just lined up like the Queen's soldiers in long rows, the odd one fainting and falling over.

There are variants too. The 'stock' cone variant seems to be more prevalent in the country lanes and appears to feed off cow manure. The 'sport event' variety possibly collects sweat or beer from humans as they pass by. But the most virulent are the standard unlabeled cones which, when left for a moment, multiply like coat hangers at the back of a wardrobe.

In fact, experts say the road cone problem is now officially a pandemic. In the last twelve months especially, the (legislative) environment has changed so much that there are now infestations on a weekly basis.

At the moment NZ roads seem to possess no immunity to the cones, so stop/go controls have been put in place at either side of the larger outbreaks. Cars are allowed to pass, but only at 30 km/hr lest a cone jump into the car and use the opportunity to spread.

Conspiracy theorists are saying that the cones are multiplying in response to the rollout of 5G.

An even more deluded theory is that they are deliberately placed on the road for traffic management purposes. Experts in the study of cones, witcheshatologists, say the latter simply could not be the case because there are now so many that no one takes any notice of them anyway.

Then, as quickly as they arrived, the rows of cones disappear. Except for a few which have escaped into a nearby ditch, someone's back yard, or the local sports field. A few have been known to climb to the top of trees, as if trying to get to road-cone heaven.

Long after the infestation has ceased, you can still see a rotting cone or two in that same ditch or lying under an abandoned car. Some think they are not dead but lying dormant ready to multiply again when conditions are ripe.

Preliminary studies of their lifecycle, indicate that when they disappear from the road most migrate en-masse to large warehouses where they hibernate, perhaps in preparation for the day when they will completely cover the roads.

Meanwhile, our leaders are asking that the public stay at home, be kind and avoid contact with the cones. They are being told that if one does appear outside their property, to call the local soccer coach or cycling club, and they will remove, neutralize, and re-purpose it.

Overseas, a rediscovered strategy called common sense is showing some success in cutting road cone numbers. NZ still appears a long way from adopting this form of treatment despite it once being in widespread use to combat a variety of scourges.

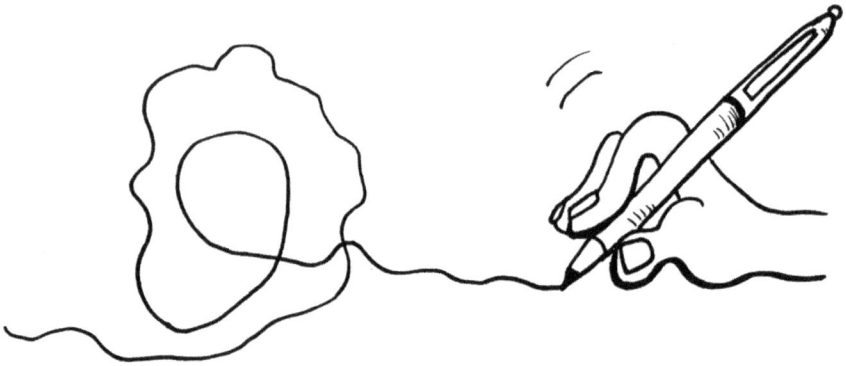

Health

Breakfast kick starts your day

An Apple A Day

Can you have your cake and eat it too?

Obesity – Your Choice?

Exercise Testing – What's good for you?

How to keep warm at no cost

The power of becoming redundant

Am I hearing you?

Te Whare Tapa Whā – applying the four health walls to our health system

Breakfast kick starts your day

This well-known phrase implies that if you don't eat breakfast, your metabolism will do a 'go-slow'. Catching a slow metabolism is about as popular as catching COVID. It's how you go from a size 10 to a 16 overnight and put on that spare tyre around your waist. And like COVID, a slow metabolism isn't your fault!

Anyway, the "kick start" thing must be true because it's written on the back of the cereal packet where all those scientific words reside: Low fat, B1, B2, folate, fibre, ironman food, and "like a chocolate milkshake only crunchy".

Taking this knowledge further, two bowls of cereal should kick start my day even better than a single bowl. Surely then if I ate three bowls I'd end up looking like an Ironman athlete in a week or so.

Well, not exactly. In fact, if you ate three bowls of processed breakfast cereal each morning you'd probably feel sluggish and full most of the day, experience nasty flatulence, and get fat quicker than you can say "B complex".

The concept that eating breakfast elevates your metabolism is sound. When you have a meal, that food needs to be digested and metabolized. Around ten percent of the energy value of that meal is used in those processes. So, compared to the fasted state in which you wake, eating breakfast certainly does increase your metabolism. Slightly. However, the other 90% of the energy content of that breakfast must be stored in the body, either as fat or carbohydrate. The cereal companies conveniently forget to mention that.

So, the notion that eating breakfast magically stops you from getting fat is complete fallacy. The "...kick starts your day" phrase is simply a great marketing line that has become dogma in a (first) world where people can afford an overly processed food product contained in a colourful box.

At this point you should be questioning that other long-held belief that "Breakfast is the most important meal of the day". Is it?

Well, it is if you are in the business of selling breakfast cereal. For the rest of us it's probably no more important than any other meal. And anyway, why do we have to eat cereal for breakfast? What's wrong with meat and three veg?

The breakfast cereal thing is just one of many examples of how the general public has been hoodwinked with clever marketing.

Another recent and salient example is the idea that electric cars produce no emissions. I've even seen the words 'Zero Emissions' written on the side of an EV. True or not?

Well, the side of the car is about as trustworthy as the cereal box when it comes to knowledge. And anyway, what sort of "emissions" are they talking about?

Building just one car requires a massive input of energy and materials, both of which result in all sorts of emissions including CO_2 and toxic waste. Then we have to get the car to NZ somehow, and that consumes energy and produces further emissions of varying amounts. Finally, to make that car move requires energy to charge the battery each day.

Currently in NZ that energy as electricity will contain at least some coal-related input. The rest might come from "renewables:", but even getting windmills up to speed produces massive amounts of CO_2 and environmental degradation.

So, the idea that you can purchase a car that has "zero emissions" is complete rubbish. It is simply a slogan developed by a clever vehicle company marketer. Sadly, many people, even those making the laws in Wellington, have been sucked in.

I'm not saying electric vehicles are not a reasonable option for getting around. But dumping your little petrol-powered hatchback and ploughing your hard earned into a new EV is not going to save the world like the car companies would have you believe.

What will be much more effective is to get rid of your big 4 x 4 if you don't really need it and be gentle on the accelerator pedal in any car you drive. Better still, avoid using a car all together when you can find an alternative like public transport.

If you really want to kick start your day, walk or ride to work. That'll increase your metabolic rate ten times more than eating breakfast and get you closer to zero emission than anything else.

And it'll probably help you lose some weight too.

An Apple A Day

A friend, after hosting my once young children for fish and chips, commented that the Stannard kids were the only ones who cried, not when the hot chips ran out, but when all the lemon slices were gone.

Even at a young age our lot had developed a taste for many different foods, and plenty of them. Now as young adults they eat and enjoy just about any food.

Taking advice from our elders, other parents, and being half sensible, we exposed our kids to a wide variety of foods and restricted processed sugary stuff from the time they were weaned. At parties, of course, they'd go berserk on cake and lollies, but that was fine as it wasn't the norm.

It was also a whole lot cheaper to give your toddler a smashed up version of what you have for dinner than buying specialised toddler foods designed with tastes and textures to get the kids hooked. And then they also eat when you eat, so the social importance of meals becomes embedded.

Outside mealtime at our place there was always fruit or veg available as a snack. There was also stuff in the garden to forage on when the adults weren't looking, including the odd half ripe plum or moth-coddled apple. Good healthy stuff.

Anyway, an apple a day, especially with a grub in it, keeps the doctor away doesn't it?

Not anymore, because for pre-schoolers, apples can only be eaten at childcare if they're shredded according to new Ministry of Health Guidelines.

These recently released recommendations are aimed at reducing the risk of food-related choking in early learning services such as early childhood education services, ngā kōhanga reo and certificated playgroups. At home as well, because these recommendations are targeted at parents too.

Most of it seems the bleeding obvious and, I hope, is in the Plunket handbook. Don't give toddlers nuts, hard lollies, chippies, Cheerios and marshmallows. Or Lego. But some of the other stuff is getting a bit precious, especially for 4-6 year olds, like quartering grapes, grating carrot and celery, and finely chopping lettuce.

A time-stretched parent of child-care kid is more likely to just buy a bag of processed fruit or salad, or even bottled meals rather than painstakingly cut up their grapes or shred the carrot. More packaging and more cost. It might also mean limiting the range of food that is provided for the child, and certainly the jaw work.

Perhaps more importantly, a child who gets used to processed food is less likely to enjoy the unprocessed equivalent when they are older. And with that in mind, I wonder if kids only exposed to mushed up food learn not to choke on stuff later in life? There is a plethora of unknowns associated with the outcome of this MoH dictum and a potential raft of ongoing health, dental, and speech issues.

What brought about this effort to dictate to the pre-schools and parents what and how to feed their kids?

The explanation is that, between 2002 and 2009, nine young children in NZ died from choking, one of these in an early childhood centre. The context of those deaths is not described, and the food itself maybe only partly to blame. Nevertheless, someone has decided that around one choking death per year is significant enough to influence the food intake of the next generation.

When the overwhelming health crisis that we face is obesity and related comorbidities, any policy making plain old fruit and vegies harder to provide at a young age, should be carefully scrutinised.

Mitigating a tiny but immediate risk to the population while producing a potentially huge but delayed risk to the future is, by definition, short-sighted.

But modern politicians seem to be statistically naive and completely risk averse. The media inflate risk to Joe Public, and bingo; another policy which serves a squeaky wheel, but simultaneously removes common-sense and personal responsibility from the equation.

Have a think for a moment what our ANZACs would have said about how our leaders now measure and manage risk.

I reckon this sort of nanny-state stuff would be hard for them to swallow.

Can you have your cake and eat it too?

There's nothing worse than being called a hypocrite.

Dictionary.com defines a hypocrite as: a person who pretends to have virtues, moral or religious beliefs, principles, etc., that he or she does not actually possess, especially a person whose actions belie stated beliefs.

So a hypocrite is someone who wants it both ways; they want their cake and they want to eat it too. A number of former American TV evangelists immediately come to mind.

So one has to be very careful when expressing an opinion lest your actions do not align.

I suspect everyone is guilty of this at some point, so it's a big call to label someone else as a hypocrite, and has been for quite a while. "He that is without sin among you, let him cast the first stone" said Jesus, according to the apostle John.

In a scientific context, a hypocrite might be someone who may present some data then contradict what that data indicates.

An example of this is when someone uses an association between variables to support a statement, then contradicts themselves by ignoring that association when it suits.

A person's maximal heart rate in beats per minute can be estimated by subtracting their age from 220. This text-book method, oft-used and accepted in the exercise industry, is based on a large data set associating heart rate and age. But the reverse is just as acceptable - that we can estimate someone's age if we know their maximal heart rate.

"Sir, your maximal heart rate is 170 beats per minute, thus you are 50 years of age", doesn't sound nearly as convincing. But it would be hypocritical to accept this prediction of maximum HR and not the estimate of age.

Large descriptive studies used in population studies for health or well-being for example, also draw associations between a range of recorded variables and a (primary) variable of interest.

Such investigations can show that variation in socio-economic position or geographical location, can explain a good deal of the variation in body fatness in NZ adults. For example, the less money that comes into your household, the more likely you are to carry more body fat.

However, association and cause are different things, so understanding the mechanisms via which such associations occur is difficult.

This is where experimental studies are required to understand, using this example, the mechanism underlying the association between income and body fat. But these studies are difficult, expensive, and ethically challenging, so they are generally not done. So, we don't completely understand why Kiwis whose household income is less are more likely to be fatter.

But sans the experimental studies, the association is often interpreted as "having less money makes you fat". Makes great media! And from there it is extrapolated that, if you can reduce the "inequality" - make poorer people richer - you can reduce the prevalence of obesity.

If we were to accept this idea, then we would also have to accept that anyone who has low body fat does so because they earn more money. It would be hypocritical not to.

Now I'd strongly suspect that all those people who have lost significant body weight without pharmacological influence would be pretty upset if told their achievement was not due to discipline or hard graft but because they began earning more money.

So, when employing statistical associations to estimate or predict characteristics of a person or group (such as body composition, income, education, indices of health etc.), one must be willing to equally accept the breadth of that association. It would be hypocritical not to.

The hard grafters at least have certainly learnt that they can't get their cake and eat it too.

Obesity - Your Choice?

Obese people recently became political footballs.

Perhaps to appeal to a portion of the still-to-vote electorate, Judith Collins declared that obesity was "a personal choice". In the dying days of her campaign, she stated that people should "entirely have to take personal responsibility and not blame the system for personal choices".

Naturally, the other (Labour) side weighed in, disagreeing and noting that the previous National govt took a science and evidence base to this issue. And as PM Ardern pointed out, the issue is "...not as simplistic as Judith Collins made out."

So what's the truth? Does obesity occur because a person isn't taking enough responsibility for their body? Or is it complex and the "the system" to blame?

Obesity and its co-morbidities have become more prevalent in NZ – we are the third fattest nation in the OCED and have the second fattest children. Something or someone else must be at fault. We are, after all, in the enlightened age of looking for someone else to blame.

Perhaps we can blame the Aussie-owned supermarkets for making the price of healthy food expensive, and crap food cheap?

Perhaps we can also blame the fast-food outlets, or the soft drink companies. 5G anyone?

Fat is the main way our bodies store energy. Generally speaking, a person puts on fat when their energy intake through food they ingest, digest and absorb, exceeds the sum of energy they expend in growth, physical activity, and just maintaining their body to stay alive.

Fat is a great way of storing energy because it doesn't mix with water and is very concentrated in energy which can be used if food is scarce. Which these days is not often.

All of us carry some fat, most of it in adipose tissue cells under our skin and around our organs. It does a few other things apart from energy storage like helping keep us warm and protecting our internal organs.

High levels of body fat indicate that a person has spent a good chunk of time, often many years, eating more energy than they expend.

Someone is obese when they carry so much body fat it is unhealthy. When this happens, their adipose tissue can't cope with storing all that fat, so it spills out into other parts of the body and causes problems such as diabetes.

To reduce body fat, you have to devote time expending more energy than you eat through doing more physical activity, eating less energy dense food, or ideally both.

So let's get back to the blame game: Energy intake versus energy expenditure.

While there is a small percentage of people who have trouble performing physical activity, the vast majority of the two-thirds of NZ adults who are overweight or obese could expend more energy through exercise or physical work. Primarily their choice.

While there is a small percentage of people who have conditions or medications which encourage them to eat too much energy, that same two-thirds of kiwi adults who are overweight or obese, could reduce how much food or drink goes into their mouth. Their choice.

So Collins is partly right. However, for someone to be able to make a choice they must be in a position where they have some control. Because without control you can't make a choice and then take responsibility!

For example, young kids don't have much control over what goes in the family shopping trolley or have access to a backyard cricket pitch. An obese child is almost certainly going to turn into an obese adult. Similarly, cooking vegies for dinner is hard if you've never learnt to cook or don't have access to a grocery shop. And you can't cycle to work on a four-lane highway chock full of cars.

For many people, education about food and nutrition is needed - providing knowledge which can help gain some control, prioritise, and shift some environmental barriers.

However, the truth is that reducing your energy intake and doing more physical activity is key. It can be damn hard to do, but that shouldn't mean it's not your responsibility.

It has become all too popular for academics to look for ways to explain our obesity issue by conjuring up ideas on how it's our environment that shapes our shape. This is not only often self-serving – "we'll get a research grant" – but it's also doing those who need to lose weight a disservice by twisting the truth. There are academics who have literally lived off the fat of the land, getting research grants to reduce obesity, failing, then getting another.

So the truth about obesity is out there – if only it were as palatable as a Big Mac.

Exercise Testing – What's good for you?

As a newbie lecturer in exercise physiology at Massey 17 years ago, the Ethics Committee at the time ruled that everyone, elite athletes included, required approval from a cardiac specialist before they could do an exercise test in our laboratory. A few Committee members believed that exercise was dangerous for the heart, and screening would reduce any risk of a heart attack occurring during university hours.

Their belief possibly came from child-hood trauma of school PE, or some old-fashioned belief that exercise is bad for you, especially women – the same misguided thinking that saw only men run the Olympic marathon until 1984. But exercise does stress the heart, and any problems with that vital organ could be exposed on the treadmill, and death could indeed occur.

The term 'Sudden Cardiac Death' (SCD) refers to an unexpected death from a cardiovascular cause that occurs without prior symptoms or within one hour of symptom onset. With SCD, even outwardly healthy people can just drop dead, although it most often relates to undetected heart disease associated with smoking, obesity, and poor diet. The unexpected nature of SCD makes it very traumatic, more so when it happens to a young person, even worse if it happens to a fine physical specimen like an athlete. The latter occurs because of an arrhythmia or undetected structural flaw with their heart and it just fails one day, sometimes during exercise. A tragic incident like that is quite emotive and becomes etched in the mind.

Exercise and sport can be dangerous, but usually from twisting an ankle or doing a hammy rather than an exercise-induced heart attack, even for the average Kiwi who is somewhat unfit and a bit fat.

In the general population, SCD occurs at the rate of about 0.035% of the population per year, higher in older people, and less in the young. In supervised exercise like sport where participants are younger and less fat, the rate is about 0.002%, and less again in the sporty people that I was wanting to test.

In fact, a lack of exercise is far more dangerous. In NZ, estimates are that lack of physical activity causes around 13% of deaths per year.

Given that 0.75% of the NZ population dies every year, that's an annual incidence of about 0.1% due to physical inactivity, about 50 times higher than having an exercise-induced heart attack in my sporty lot.

Sensibly most modern health professionals understand such statistics and often prescribe exercise even for older people recovering from a heart attack because it improves cardiac function, reduces the chance of further problems, and improves quality of life.

But old beliefs and social media rumours die hard, inviting many to still believe exercise is dangerous. And because unfitness, obesity and heart disease are so common, they become expected and are an acceptable means of death. On the other hand, dropping dead young because you inherited a dodgy ticker, even though it's extremely rare, is not.

For some on my learned Ethics Committee, emotions were far more powerful than statistics when weighing up risk, so it took nearly a year of dialogue before I could do an exercise test on anyone but myself.

Right now in NZ it is crucial that emotions and media hype don't take precedence over good evidence-based data collection and analysis when we decide what action to take to deal with the virus.

Interestingly, the annual mortality rate attributed to smoking in NZ is 0.1% of the population. That is, we'd need 5,000 people to die from COVID-19 this year to match smoking in 2020 alone. And while we are thankfully keeping a lid on the virus by stopping people flying into NZ, we can still buy fags at the airport, duty free.

How to keep warm at no cost

As an exercise physiologist, my research involved conducting experiments with humans.

When developing or testing a methodology I always made sure that my body was involved, partly to make sure it was safe, partly so I could iron out the methods, and partly so I could describe to potential study participants what it would be like.

Whilst a PhD student I also "donated" my body to other students' research, because they might have reciprocated. And anyway, there is no better way to learn cutting edge stuff than to get intimately involved in another's study.

Over time I experienced muscle biopsies, various muscle probes, electric shocks, starvation, ECGs, EEGs, and many hours feeling claustrophobic in MRI machines. Oh, and then there were the (literal) litres of blood, sweat and urine that was collected from my person during exercise and at rest.

It was all very interesting, and usually fun – when it was over.

One of the most uncomfortable studies I participated in, that of another PhD student, was when we tried to heat the body core up using externally applied heat.

The idea was to put people into a hot bath, with a raincoat on no less, and keep adding hot water until we got the body temperature up to around 39.5 degrees Celsius. Normal internal body temperature is about 37 degrees, so two degrees doesn't sound like much but it's hard to achieve by applying heat from the outside.

So much so that I was pulled out at well under 39 degrees (from memory) because I got so agitated and swore so much at my colleagues that they, perhaps rightly, thought I was losing my marbles.

They got most of the data they wanted though, because the temperature probes in my muscles indicated close to medium rare.

Anyhow, the lesson I learnt from that, apart from never again volunteering for a similar study, was that it's really hard to heat the body up through externally applied heat.

On the other hand, during exercise it's much easier to get body core temperature to near 39 degrees, and considerably easier again to get a working muscle temperature to that level.

For example, even on a very cold day, try walking down a long steep hill then feel your thigh muscles when you reach the bottom. They will be hot for reasons much like why the brakes of your car heat up when stopping the vehicle.

Then try walking back up the hill with your puffer jacket on and zipped up. You'll have beads of sweat on your forehead by the top and the puffer will be off. The warmth that you feel at that point is coming from within; primarily a product of your muscles' metabolism and what scientists call Entropy. It's the same reason your car engine heats up as you drive it.

We have had some cold snaps recently and it's made me think about the best way to keep warm.

Sitting in front of a heater or a fire is a pretty inefficient way of getting your body warm because it's using externally applied heat. Sure, that warmth will provide a pleasant feeling on your skin – until you move away from it. Going into a warm room or whole house with the heat pump going will also be pleasant, and if you stay there for some time you will eventually warm up. But heat pumps don't come cheap and then they cost to run. Then there is the carbon cost.

A very much more efficient, and cheaper way to get your body warm is to create heat from within by putting your muscles to work. Go for a run or brisk walk in your warm clothes – the faster the better. If you can't do that, do some push-ups or sit-ups on the loungeroom floor. Jump up and down on the spot, or do the vacuuming. Then once you've had enough and want to watch TV, wrap yourself in a big blanket to conserve that body warmth for as long as possible.

Shivering is just the same. It's an involuntary contraction of your major muscle groups that forces them to work and thus produce heat through Entropy in an attempt to increase body temperature. But shivering is unpleasant and only kicks in when you get really cold. The idea is to not get to that point in the first place.

Having said all that – and I now know from personal experience – it's not possible for many people to exercise to the point where they can keep warm. They may not have the muscular strength to do it in the first place. These are the people that need good clothing and a warm environment to conserve the little heat their own body creates.

The aged and infirm are those at most risk, and these days this group are less likely to afford good clothing and a heat pump.

Nevertheless, there are few excuses for a healthy and physically capable person not to save some money by getting active, engaging with Entropy, and keeping warm!

The power of becoming redundant

Over the past five or six years I've used my expertise as a former cyclist and academic to do a bit of coaching.

It's more an "art" than a science, although being a professor in exercise physiology has certainly helped in understanding why things are done, not just what.

A number of my charges have tasted competitive success, with some ending up as National Champions, competing in World Championships, and a few even going onto full professional careers in Europe. Success from my perspective though was whether the athlete enjoyed the journey and whether they became a better person from my input.

My coaching philosophy is that a coach ought to make him/herself redundant. Meaning that, after coaching an athlete for some time, that athlete should be able to coach themselves. They should have learnt enough from me, and about themselves, so that they know what training to undertake to meet their goals and know how best to prepare for competition. At some point they then should be able to coach someone else if they choose and put something back into the sport.

It's a sort of succession planning, it's empowering for the athlete, and in any case, I could get run over by a bus some day.

That's not to say that my input might still not be useful; advice here and there, a bit of guidance and string-pulling still helps.

There are plenty of coaches who work the opposite way. They try to make themselves more essential to the athlete as time goes by, not empowering the athlete but keeping their "recipes" secret. For that coach it might be a bit of an ego thing, and if they are getting paid, it's shoring up an income.

What you then get is a dependency of the athlete on the coach, and then it's really hard if the coach/athlete relationship falls apart or breaks up for some other reason. How often do you see a sudden decrement in athlete performance when the coach disappears?

So the key to continual improvement is that the athlete is continually learning, becoming empowered, and taking responsibility. Responsibility for performance improvement, taking the kudos for winning and not blaming others when they don't.

Coaching is not confined to competitive sport. Most of the things you learn in life are from a coach in the broader context, whether that coach be mum, dad, kaumatua, other whanau, friends, or teachers. Learning how to take care of yourself, to live a healthy lifestyle is pretty much the same as learning to be good at sport.

Good parenting and/or guardianship will teach you how to live so that you are empowered to make good decisions and become a responsible adult.

A health system which does not empower a person is always going to be costly and fail. That approach is like the bad coach - it just encourages dependence on that system and allows it to become more important. It does not develop a person who takes responsibility for their own health, but reinforces that there is a solution to every health problem in a pill bottle.

On the other hand, a health system which takes an educative approach is future proofing – the preventative approach, one that engenders responsibility.

I believe that our national health system, like a good coach, should have a blue-sky goal of making itself largely redundant. With the foundation based on primary prevention, it should teach people about themselves, so they can meet their health goals, and know how best to prepare for later life. At some point in time they then should be able to teach the next generation how to live a healthy life.

That's not to say that a blue-sky health system would never be useful, providing advice here and there, and swiftly dealing with important health issues if they arise, like our "redundant" coach.

Changes were recently mooted for the NZ health system to make it more efficient and more effective. Hopefully these are aimed at empowering Kiwis to take responsibility for their own health and well-being. But if empowered and responsible, you can then no longer blame "the system" if the results don't go your way.

Am I hearing you?

I was once a poor Masters student in Sydney, living on porridge.

To borrow a phrase from some other writer, "It was the best of times and the worst of times". Pre-children and marriage, so no dependents or responsibilities, an easy part-time job, getting educated, and chasing your dreams of winning bicycle races.

On the other hand, juggling Uni and making ends meet, as well as the long training hours elite cycling requires, meant that it was stressful at times.

The borrowed house I was living in had an old phone; a now-extinct analogue type with a hand set containing a speaker at one end and a microphone at the other. The handset was connected to the rest of the phone and a dial through a curly cord.

Being right-handed I usually listened to the caller through my right ear. But one fateful day I swapped sides mid-call and the volume decreased dramatically. Swapping back to the right side, I immediately realized that I'd lost a good deal of hearing in my left ear. What's more, when I tried to listen hard on my left side, a high-pitched ringing noise would be there. Suddenly the price of porridge oats was not high on my agenda.

A quick trip to my GP produced a referral to one of the best-known specialists in Sydney. However, to get in quickly rather than wait months on the public list, would cost me about $200. At that time $200 amounted to about my life savings, but finding the cause of my fairly sudden hearing loss and tinnitus was important. And anyway, I could just forgo the brown sugar on my porridge for the next 200 years and that'd pay for it.

Off I trotted to the specialist. After a battery of tests and observations, the wise old gentleman told me that I have a conductive hearing loss and that it could be operated on. But, he said, "we'd only do that if you stopped riding your bicycle".

I assume he was saying that he didn't want to waste his time doing an operation on someone who might fall off their bike, rattle their head, and undo his good work.

If the census over there had asked me at the time what culture I'd identified as, it would be a 'Cyclist'. That's how important my sport and related way of life was to me back then. And anyway, I didn't have a car, so biking was how I got around.

So, the decision between cycling and a conductive hearing loss was an easy one for me. In any case, perhaps sometime in the future I would stop riding and get it done then. And anyway, a conductive hearing loss didn't need urgent treatment and wasn't a death sentence.

Thirty years later and I'm still deaf in that ear. Perhaps surgical methods or medical attitudes have changed by now and a younger me wouldn't now be put in that conundrum?

Imagine an optometrist telling some young cricketer that he would not prescribe a new set of glasses unless she stopped facing the fast bowlers? Or that a woman suffering from alopecia couldn't get a wig subsidy because she was always seeing her mokopuna and they might damage it.

Our government has made a big and expensive call in establishing Te Aka Whai Ora, the new Māori Health Authority. It's been formed to improve the health outcomes of Māori, presumably by providing equality of health care access by embedding a Māori cultural context. I can see the benefits of this to Māori who experience higher rates of conditions like heart disease and diabetes.

My hearing experience is a good lesson to me about what people consider important in their journey to optimal health and well-being, especially within their cultural context. Because what's at the top of the list of importance to one person, including the provider, might not be at the top of the list to another.

Having now spent quite a bit of time in the "bowels" of the NZ health system with an on-going health issue I've observed where some of the stresses and strains in that system lie.

Much of these concern a lack of funding or access to appropriately trained expertise. I'm sure there are rate-limiting physical and geographical issues in resource availability too. Whether it's the two-month wait to see your GP, lack of drug options for many cancer patients, or simply not enough doctors or nurses for surgery, money has a big role to play.

In the health system, decisions influenced by insufficient money can be close to a death sentence for some people and certainly make life miserable.

So, while I understand the immense importance that culture can play in personal health and well-being, there are some basic problems in NZ Health that need dealing with. These have life and death consequences for all cultural groups in our country.

Let's hope Te Aka Whai Ora works well for all of us, not just a minority.

But meanwhile let's sort out the basic and important issues in Health NZ as soon as possible.

Te Whare Tapa Whā – applying the four health walls to our health system

There's nothing like a cancer diagnosis to make you think about what is important in your life. It also makes you think about why you drew the short straw, including what aspect of your living to date has contributed to bad luck.

Managing the disease then, makes you think about what constitutes good health and well-being, and that's where Sir Mason Durie's interpretation, 'Te Whare Tapa Whā' makes good reading.

It's a Māori paradigm that describes the foundation of well-being as having four equal sides, like a whare or house.

These are: taha tinana (physical health), taha wairua (spiritual health), taha whānau (family health), and taha hinengaro (mental health).

Now I'm not an expert on the in-depth understanding of these, but the gist of it makes sense to me. And you don't have to be a rocket scientist (nor an expert in mātauranga Māori) to be confident that there's more to health than just the physical bit. This model tells us exactly that.

"Happy wife, happy life" for a start.

Yet, the way we still measure and approach health in NZ is, by-and-large, just physical. And people are treated in our health system, by-and-large, on physical measures. I guess that's the "Western" health and medical model, one we've adopted, and it certainly shores up one wall of the whare.

However, if there were links between physical and mental/spiritual/family health and we were only dealing with the physical, imagine how much better our collective well-being would be if we considered the other three sides of the whare.

So are there links between these?

Firstly, you can only associate or link variables if you have them measured. As they say, if you don't measure it, it doesn't exist. But if you don't think it's important you probably won't measure it.

There should be plenty of data relating to the 'side' of mental health, including stress, but family and spiritual health data are harder to come by.

Acute emotional stress has, for a long time, been linked to sudden cardiovascular events like heart attacks, although the effect of chronic stress on physical well-being, and specifically the development of cardiovascular disease, is only more recently getting attention.

These data are suggesting that if a person experiences stress because of things such as divorce, death in the family, prolonged illness, unwanted change of residence, natural catastrophe, or a highly competitive work situation, then they are at greater risk of suffering from cardiovascular disease. Of course other factors, such as obesity and inactivity are also linked to cardiovascular disease, and it's possible stress is somehow linked directly to a lifestyle that produces those too.

Cancer, another big killer in NZ, appears to have some association with experience of stress, at least according to research done elsewhere.

Without experimental studies on stress and disease, research which would be ethically impossible to do, we can only speculate as to the reason behind these associations. Studies in rodents deliberately exposed to "social defeat" which produces stress, do show increased systemic and local inflammation, and this tilts some biological processes towards cancer development.

Regardless, we could fairly confidently predict that removing, or at least dealing with stressful situations has a better chance of reducing the incidence of cardiovascular disease and cancer than doing nothing at all.

Lastly, data from the NZ Ministry of Health webpages note that suicide was the third leading cause of death for Māori males and the second leading cause of death for non-Māori males between 2010 and 2012. This is clearly a mental health issue and, I suspect, has not improved much in the decade or so since then.

All of this should give some weight to Sir Mason Durie's health model (Sir Mason developed the four-wall house model in 1984), and you could argue that the model should provide some guidance as to how we define and deal with health and well-being in our society.

Our biggest potential health issue for the time being is COVID. Potential, because very few people have actually died in NZ with the virus. But if it does get a hold in the community, many more will.

The way it's been controlled, especially across the ditch using the coarse tool of a lockdown, is a numbers game based on minimizing infection; physical health. Our "experts" would argue that it is the only initial combat tool worth using. Perhaps it is.

In the post-analysis that must take place once COVID-19 is under control, I assume the mental, spiritual, or family aspects of well-being will be considered. However, if we don't have the data relating to those three sides of the whare we will never know the full impact that the battle of COVID has had on us.

So I trust that our government is collecting that data, because I expect them to understand that health isn't just physical and people aren't just numbers.

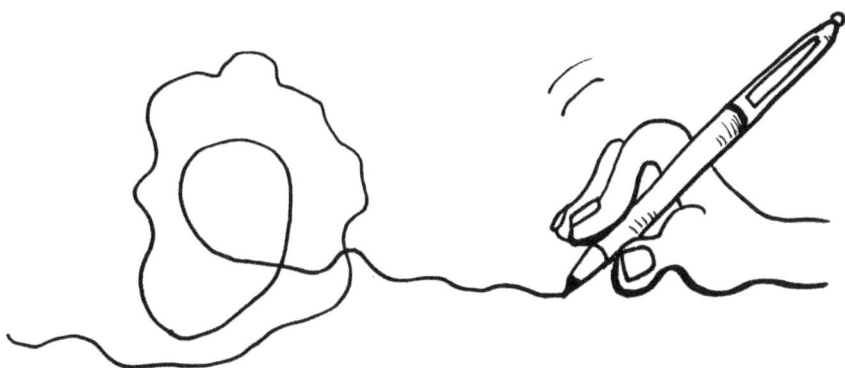

Environment

Gravity, a force we take for granted

Rates – money for jam

Nero and all that...

Houston, we have a problem! CO_2 is increasing rapidly

Gravity, a force we take for granted

There are times during various medical treatment regimes when I've become so weak it's simply hard to stand up.

Quite a contrast from my first 50 years when the ability to run around, carry things, or pick heavy things up wasn't something you had a second thought about.

Just at the moment, bending down is hard. Getting up from the floor is really hard work. I know there are many people who have experienced or are experiencing the same thing. I imagine it's what happens when you get old too.

Every time I drop something I swear, because I then need to somehow get down and pick it up. Arms and good flexibility help get the job done but it's an extra effort and painful.

Me versus gravity. Steve versus 9.8 m/s2.

Gravity is something we take for granted.

Our bodies are energy-hungry. Just to keep us alive we need energy, from food, to enable our nervous system to work, maintain pressure in our blood vessels and to keep warm. When we are asleep, that's where our energy goes. But as soon as we get up and about, most of the energy we expend is used to fight gravity.

Just standing up, for a start, requires postural muscles to work and expend energy to keep our skeleton erect. Then we need to move our bodies, ventilate, digest, and do a whole lot of other stuff which requires some physical work against gravity.

Moving around is the big one, walking, running, and other forms of locomotion require plenty of muscular work, which requires chemical energy from food. This is why weight-bearing exercise is prescribed to burn energy (read: fat) because gravity is hungry, energy wise. And it's why weight supported exercise like pool work is not nearly as effective in getting rid of that spare tyre.

Thinking more broadly; want to take a trip to Auckland? Most of that carbon you are going to create in the car, on the train, and in the air, is going to counter gravity to get over the lumps and bumps of terrain. Flying is a little different because you are creating CO2 for the convenience of speed as well, but it takes massive amounts of fuel to get an aeroplane full of people to 20,000 feet.

Further, think of building a house or multi-story apartment. Getting the foundations built, the services installed, and then all that stuff that goes on top; most of the fuel spent doing that is working against gravity. That's after fighting gravity to get all the materials on site, sometimes from the other side of the world.

We have some smart ways of capturing energy to fight gravity, sometime using gravity itself!

We can stop the water reaching the ocean with a dam, halfway along the gravity "train". Then we get 'one over' gravity when we let that water out and generate power from that last few metres drop to sea level, power that we can use against gravity. It's clever, fairly green, and cost effective. When it rains!

Imagine if we could just dial gravity back, not all the way, say to about half, just for an hour or two per day. We could get a whole lot of stuff done quickly in that time and probably meet our carbon targets easily.

Between, 10 and noon, we could quickly fill the logging trucks, pour the cement up onto the 5th story, pick up a fallen pylon, or lay some train tracks. Just schedule it in. We could pump some water up to a dam with less energy and then let it down later to produce more than we spent.

All of us who drop stuff like socks and clothesline pegs can do that in the morning and not get so frustrated because the physical effort of picking them up at "low gravity hour" would be less.

Of course there are going to be down-sides like bad hair and sideways rain, but only temporarily. And we would need to postpone if there was the threat of a storm surge.

But I reckon the idea has legs and you heard it here first.

I'll give Elon a call.

Rates – money for jam

We live in a decent sized section in Palmerston North city. It's a back section, so a good chunk of that is driveway, but since the footprint of our house is not big, there is plenty of lawn to mow and space for a vegetable garden.

When the kids were young there was space to kick a ball, throw a Frisbee, and have water fights on a rare hot day. The kids even constructed their own mountain bike track around the front yard, destroying the garden along the way.

These days, it's less busy outside, but my wife and I still enjoy the space, growing some natives, exotics, vegies, and composting waste from the café. Excess fruit and vegies, and even compost, gets given to friends and neighbours. A seasonal glut of fruit is made into jam when time allows, and most of that is given to friends.

If we ever had to be self-sufficient for food we could go close some of the year, although I'd have to get my fix of dairy from someone with a cow.

The big family-friendly section is one reason that, as ex-Sydneysiders, we decided to call Palmerston North home. It has been, looking back, a great place to raise our kids.

Around us now though, nearly all the other larger sections have been dissected and re-developed to contain two modern houses. Some have been trisected, or more.

But when you look at our house on Google Maps, our roof is one of the smaller in the suburb, while our section is larger than average. The footprint of recently built houses is much bigger, and the concrete driveway and parking pad make up the rest of the section.

So, the old quarter acre sections in town often now have two houses with a quarter acre of roof and concrete driveway between them. With no garden to soak up rain - it's not just climate change that's increasing flash-flooding and river water quality issues.

These new houses have just enough room down the side to move a wheelie bin or access the power box. Certainly nowhere to swing a cricket bat. Or a cat.

Goodness knows what the kids of the house will do when they are not at school? They can only shoot so many hoops on the obligatory basketball ring nailed to the front of the obligatory double garage. Perhaps kids now just play video games in the obligatory entertainment room? Anyway, they won't be learning to bunny-hop their BMX in the front yard. Backyard rugby? Nah.

And growing vegies in these infill houses would be a seriously challenging pastime, although I have seen clever people make good use of pots and a warm micro-climate that a steel fence and a concrete pad can produce. Even those people need to buy feijoas.

Currently there is great kerfuffle about the magnitude of proposed rates rises for some residents. In our case, we are looking at an increase of about 20% because of the perceived increased value of our land.

It has risen in value, I'm guessing, because of the potential to make money by dividing the section and building another house.

City councils love this sort of development because they will get two lots of rates where there was previously one. And they don't have to spend that extra money earned on the footpath or roadway out the front. For them it's money for jam.

However, from where I'm sitting, we are being penalised by the council for owning a biggish section. It feels like the rate rise is a deliberate move to force us to sub-divide and contribute to the infill housing solution.

When presented with my new rates invoice, the question will be, "What extra value or service am I getting from council for that extra $900 per year you are asking me to pay?"

I'm pretty sure they'll not be able to answer that. Nor will they have thought through the consequences of rampant infill on the environment, the neighbourhood, let alone a play space for future generations. We are, after all, only custodians of the land for the present, and once the green space is gone, it's gone.

In a city with population growth, there must be many other solutions which provide for a dwelling to be built. Just not in my backyard.

We'll hold off sub-dividing for as long as we can afford to because I want someone else in the future to have the space to raise active children like we did. But meanwhile I'll have to sell my jam to pay for the rates increase rather than give it away.

Jam for money!

Nero and all that...

A few year ago I nick-named my then teenage daughter, 'the environmental vandal'. Coined because, like many teenagers I suppose, she would luxuriate in long hot showers, never turn a light off, and insist on us buying expensive imported items when the locally-produced thing was available at half the price. To her I was the tight-arse dad who ran around turning off lights, drove a daggy old car, and rode my bike to work. Unlike her friends' fathers, who apparently all drove new beamers, wore Italian suits, and must have owned the electricity company. I did work out that it saved me $10 every time I rode to work, which probably just offset the electricity bill when my daughter was home, but the greenie in me did derive some self-satisfaction from contributing to the climate cause.

So it was to my surprise that, the other day, my now 22-year-old contacted me from Melbourne to say that she'd been to a climate change rally. And she had even decided that she personally needed to change a few things in her life because climate change was actually a thing and, "we all have to contribute in a small way to fight it". There were 150,000 people protesting there, mostly kids, and you can bet they were all worried about what the world might look like for them when they reach the ripe old age of 30.

While Melbourne and its surrounds cop a hammering with extreme heat, drought, and bush fires, here in the Manawatū, apart from the odd downpour or cold snap, climate change so far hasn't affected us. So when the boffins start talking about sea-level rises of 50 cm it's easy to go glassy-eyed and keep dropping the kids off at the school gate in the big SUV. And even if we do believe, we can just blame the farmers again, while we drive to the supermarket to get (their) food. Yet around the world, climate-related change is really happening and people are taking action.

So what can we do here to save the planet? The NZ Ministry for the Environment says that one of the easiest things you can do is ride or walk instead of driving a car. Cars alone are the reason that NZ household greenhouse gas emissions have risen by 20% in the last 10 years (ref Statistics NZ).

In London, bike lanes and pedestrian-only areas have taken over many roads, Paris is now lime-scooter green, and in Rome they are legislating to only allow development around public transit nodes to minimize car use.

Meanwhile in Palmerston North, councillors, publicly supportive of sustainable transport (cycling, scooters and walking), are flinching over the reaction of a few to the loss of some on street carparking in College St to make way for a safe cycle lane. Loss of this public space, for their personal use, would leave some residents without a kerbside parking spot outside their house - despite the fact that they all have their own driveways and off-street parking garages! And the debate has been going on for three years.

So while London, Paris, and Rome take action to stop the world from burning, here, we fiddle.

Houston, we have a problem! CO2 is increasing rapidly

I'm not a climate change expert. I've not read the best scientific publications concerning how the activities of humans have affected climate change.

So, I will have to trust the 'experts' who say that we must do our best to reduce our CO2 emissions. That means reducing our reliance on fossil fuels which release CO2 as they release energy for us to use.

Nevertheless, I do like to try to understand a topic to be able to form an educated opinion, especially if there are dissenting voices and claims of conspiracy.

With a good science education under my belt, I am confident I can get the gist of things like CO2 and I know how to get up-to-date information from a variety of reliable sources.

I can see online what NASA is recording as the trend in atmospheric CO2 concentration over the last 20 years or so, and it's clearly up. Average temperatures have increased in tandem. Whether or not they are related has produced some argument; association does not prove causation.

Now you have to remember that this is NASA, from the country of oil tycoons and massive SUVs, so I strongly suspect there is no CO2 conspiracy there.

Taking an experimental approach – one needed to prove causation - you can show that increasing CO2 concentration will enable air to trap a bit more heat. Then when liquid water is available, like oceans, the water content of the air increases and that moisture traps more heat again. So CO2 is a sort of catalyst for increasing air temperature.

Houston, we have a problem!

Studies of ancient ice samples suggest that over millions of years atmospheric CO2 concentrations have gone up and down around some sort of equilibrium. In other words, if they go up over a few million years, then they'll go down a few million years later, naturally.

Maybe that's because when CO2 and water vapour concentrations are high and the air temperature is warm, plants grow more readily and store that CO2 over time. Over a very long time, that will be as peat, oil, and coal.

So you ask, if CO2 is increasing then at some point it will decrease and we'll be sweet? That's right, it probably will - in about twenty million years. Meanwhile sea levels are rising a bit quicker than that and we can't wait for all those pines we are planting to turn to coal. So, the only thing we can really do is to reduce how much CO2 goes into the air, especially from the burning of fossil fuels.

In NZ we are struggling to keep our 'clean and green' image because our emissions have been increasing when others have turned theirs around. We have a majority government trying to reign in our CO2 emissions. They are going full tilt, and don't spare the horses (or the utes).

Mixed with some mainstream and social media stirring, they've managed to rile a few groups, notably owners of 4x4s, many of whom are farmers.

At this point, I'll have to disclose that I own a 4x4 ute, albeit a vintage one that only gets a short drive once or twice a week.

So, what does the science tell us about CO2 and utes?

Transport-related CO2 emissions have continued to rise here in the last decade and this has coincided with a huge rise in popularity of large 4x4s. These were once the preserve of farmers, but thanks to clever marketing they are now the vehicle of choice for tradies, soccer mums, and florists. That their CO2 production per km travelled is high compared to smaller cars, means it is sensible is discourage unnecessary use.

The government has gone straight for the jugular with a tax on purchase, but other strategies such as weight or length-limited parking spots in town may have been a better targeted policy. I bet if you legislated only yellow, pink, or lime green paint for 4x4s you'd halve their popularity overnight and also find out who really needed that size and traction.

So, the "ute tax" is a simple strategy for reducing unnecessary CO2 emissions. Unfortunately, it has come at the same time as a bunch of other rules which will affect and possibly cost, many farmers. And some political stirring has combined all these issues into what has been framed as an anti-farming agenda.

Of course, there are some other factors which are contributing to a warming atmosphere, notably methane, and unfortunately some of that is related to meat, wool, and dairy production. Unlike CO2, methane is short-lived, but 'the experts' say that reducing its production will help. Nevertheless, I'm still going to enjoy wearing my woolen undies and eating the occasional steak.

Ultimately though, to reduce CO2 emissions we need to be a society which produces and uses energy more carefully. And that means all of us, not just those who drive utes.

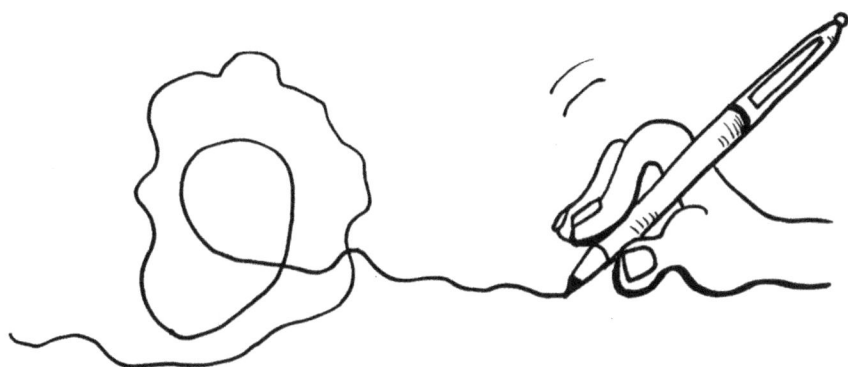

History and Culture

Cancelling Culture

There is much being made of the wave of young Kiwis heading overseas this year. Many will be doing a delayed OE, but a good few will also be leaving for better paid jobs and experience they can't get here. One day they will come back; I hope.

When I came to NZ as a young'ish academic 20 years ago I quickly worked out that NZ wasn't the place to be if you wanted to win a Nobel Prize. The people, the money, and the resources are just not here to do the sort of cutting-edge research needed. They've never been; just ask Alan McDiarmid or Earnest Rutherford our NZ Nobel Laureates, who lived elsewhere to do their ground-breaking research.

But you come to live here because it's a great place to live and breathe, and in Palmerston North, a great place to raise a family. But then it's almost inevitable that your children will leave, at least for a while, to broaden their horizons.

I have two adult children in Europe plying their trade, doing things that they couldn't do here. I've not seen them for a long time, but hopefully before the end of the year I might. Whether they will ever return to NZ to live I don't know.

Bright young things leaving means ideas, expertise, and enthusiasm goes. It puts a hole in our tax take too. More critically, there is a positivity about young adults, and when that goes the lights get a little dimmer.

If NZ Inc. like any big organization, was having such a loss of valuable young talent overseas, someone would be asking some pretty hard questions of 'The Board' about the opportunities or workplace culture. Hopefully someone in Govt is doing so.

A more important question is, how do you get them to consider coming home and bringing that talent, broadened horizons, and hard-earned cash back to Aotearoa?

Hiding from COVID worked for a bit, until it became clear that the dreaded virus was going to come here anyway – just in a delayed fashion – and while they were away NZ had become one of the most expensive places in the world to buy a house or food in relation to wage-earning capacity.

Perhaps more critically, to attract and retain, you have a to have a place where there is a decent job and plenty to see and do outside work. Sure, we have spectacular mountains and beaches, but frankly so do other places. And once you've been to Queenstown half a dozen times, you don't need to go back.

So, we need 'happening things'. On a national scale think World of Wearable Arts, the 'Wings' airshows, grapevine concerts, and international sporting events. Stuff that's entertaining, and a little different each year.

Local events might be even more important for attracting and retaining people, especially to the regions. Does a town have a good indoor swimming pool for the kids with lessons available? Is there an active hockey club with a turf, and a swath of football fields? What are the close-to-town walking tracks like? Are there some good pubs and dance venues?

But so many activities and events have been cancelled during the last two years that many of these local goings-on have been curtailed. Some clubs have ceased to exist.

On top of that, the very risk averse nature of our law-makers has made organizing events, especially those using public spaces like roads, nigh impossible.

For example, many cycling, triathlon, running, or other vehicle-related events requiring even a little bit of road space have been cancelled. The reason being that Waka Kotahi (NZTA) are now so "safety conscious" that the required traffic management is outside the financial reach of anyone but professional outfits and large roading firms.

I'm told even Santa is considering not coming for his yearly parade because his chief elf doesn't hold the requisite new traffic management qualifications!

I feel like the last two and a half years have extinguished the enthusiasm to create vibrancy through a combination of fatigue, fear, and new 'rules', the latter of which are proclaimed with no end-date. Constrictive rules without an end in sight forebode a future that's not exciting or compelling.

If we are going to attract and retain people to NZ, especially the provinces, then we need to be encouraging events and activities that create vibrancy, rather than making it more difficult. But it's so easy now not to organize them because there are too many hoops to jump through.

It's a sort of 'cancel culture' that has insidiously crept into our lives and needs to be unraveled from the highest level if we are to return to being seen as one of the world's most livable places. A place where the young and aspiring want to live.

A tale of two tales

Although I'm a naturalized Kiwi, as are my kids, I was born in Aussie and still take an interest in what's happening over there. It'll be my first overseas trip too, when our borders are open to them across the Tasman.

It took about 15 years of being away from Australia and a bit of spare time before I took an interest in its history.

Sure I'd studied a few bits of Australian past at primary school – The local mob, Captain Cook, the convict colonies, the Federation. The (aboriginal) 'dreamtime' and indigenous history was not a big part of the curriculum 40 years ago, but I understand it's appreciated more now.

A couple of months on the couch afforded by cancer treatment a few years ago prompted me to learn more about the country of my birth. And courtesy of the Red Cross book sale, 'A short history of Australia' by the late Manning Clark, an acclaimed Australian historian, became available. What's more, my mother knew him, so the ducks lined up for me to know more about where I came from.

It was an interesting and educational read, as much for the way it was written as the content. Many of the descriptions of persons of historical interest seemed to be flavoured by the author, their character in particular, and even second-guessing what they thought and thus their motives for what became important decisions.

I get it that the interest of many in human history is about behaviour, but I found Manning Clark's work, disappointingly, 'Shakespearean' in nature rather than an account of the facts. Nevertheless, I learnt a lot, and began to appreciate that, as Mark Twain noted, "The very ink with which all history is written is merely fluid prejudice".

My sister in Sydney, an historical curator of note, suggested I read a more modern narrative by another author to get a more objective view of the past, so she sent me a copy of Stuart McKintyre's 'A Concise History of Australia'. Less, in my mind at least, burdened by opinion, that historical account was a less prejudiced look at what made Australia what it is today.

Nevertheless, I'm glad I read both, and now appreciate more about how a decision made 150 years ago affects the now. After all, isn't that why knowing history is important?

At the moment there seems to be a penchant for toppling statues and banning movies made when cultural norms were different. The city of Hamilton has recently removed a statue of British naval captain John Hamilton, whom the city is named after.

Suddenly things related to those people the statues/movies represent are no longer acceptable because they are associated with an injustice or worse. I could understand why Ngai Tahu might take a dim view if a statue of Te Rauparaha was erected in Akaroa for example. But banning an episode of Fawlty Towers because it might upset the Germans? Don't mention the war, whatever you do!

I cannot see how erasing history and historical figures helps any understanding of the past, especially if there was grief or wrong-doing. Ideally people should be able to make up their own mind about what history represents, and then even if they are well educated, that is likely to be different to each.

Most importantly, as Sai Zhenzhu (Pearl Buck) said "If you want to understand today, you have to search yesterday".

So why not just knit a beanie with a pom-pom and put it on Captain Hamilton's head? That'd say more than removing him all together, and both sides of the story would be acknowledged daily.

ANZAC Birdsongs –
Do the people of Australia and NZ reflect their environment?

We came to NZ from Australia some 21 years ago. It's been an especially good move in relation to rearing children and having the opportunity to get involved in the community. Perhaps not so much for career opportunities or cutting-edge health care.

Australia and NZ are broadly similar in terms of culture and behaviour, though differences certainly exist. Some are contrasting and hit you in the face. Others are quite subtle and you can't see them until you've been back in the other country for a visit.

I reckon those dissimilarities in behaviour partly reflect the geology of the countries.

NZ behaviour tends to have a short-term focus, much like the constantly evolving land around an active fault line. We don't tend to do things with permanence, with our short-cut, she'll be right attitude, 'Number 8 wire thinking' where near enough is good enough. In Australia, the geology is old and moves slowly. People there tend to be more geographically settled, like their rocks, and subsequently build things to last.

I further my hypothesis that our behaviour reflects our natural fauna too. Whether that is through the geology of each place or whether we just mimic the animals we share our land with. Maybe it's a bit of both.

The various birds in the two countries provide a great example of how we differ as a people. We'll ignore the other animals over there, snakes, crocodiles and spiders included, because we only have birds over here with which to compare. Some would, however, suggest that those death-dealing animals mimic how Aussies conduct themselves at times, but inferring that might cause a reverse underarm response.

Anyhow, a recent trip back to Oz highlighted for me the bird thing.

We were awakened in the morning on various occasions by the loud chattering of small birds in the trees and the laughing of kookaburras.

Up high in the blue sky you can hear the faraway caw of the 'bogan' crows, and down low the colourful argumentative parrots squawking over who gets to sit where.

There is nothing modest about Aussie birds, nor are they self-conscious. They just go about their days doing their thing seemingly not worried about what else is going on around them or what anyone thinks about them. They are often very "colourful" in many senses of the word, and keen to be seen.

Most of the birds of Aotearoa, on the other hand, poke around on the forest floor with their heads down, in their own world, and oblivious to what's happening above. There is the odd exception like the kereru, which flies full throttle at low altitude, dangerously and sometimes seemingly drunk. And the bossy male tui flitting from one flowering flax to the next picking fights with his medallion-wearing contenders.

You would not consider NZ birds colourful like the Australian birds, and certainly not rowdy. Our birds are mostly black, grey, or brown, blending into their surroundings and not wanting to stand out. Maybe they are weary of putting their head up and getting it shot off?

Now it would be difficult to test my hypothesis that the behaviour of people either side of 'the ditch' reflects that of birds. Firstly, because the NZ birds would probably baulk at being study participants, and secondly, Aussie birds just wouldn't care to be involved.

On the other hand, us humans here in NZ are quite happy to refer to ourselves as kiwis and dress in grey and black like our namesake.

In Australia they'd call me a 'galah' just for coming up with the idea. And they'd call me cocky if I was brazen enough to think I was right.

The true meaning of Haka

When I was growing up in Sydney, the father of my friends next door was from Auckland. I learnt a little bit about NZ as a youngster from him and his relatives who used to visit.

One of the standout memories of him was an explanation of the "dance" the All Blacks did before each rugby match. Living deep in Sydney rugby league territory, rugby union wasn't something I knew about, but the "dance" by the "black team" was.

Since living here I've learnt more about both rugby union and the haka, and I now have some understanding of the cultural significance of an animated haka such as Ka Mate and the story it tells. It's certainly special.

To win at the highest level, the players' physiology (fitness and health) has to be optimal and the All-Blacks work very hard at that. It's also vital to be psychologically on top of your game.

As we have oft been told, winning is as much psychology as it is physiology.

Cleverly, and on the physiological side, a pre-match haka is a warm-up routine that gets the All Blacks adrenaline going and the blood flowing. Meanwhile the other team has been suckered into standing there in a huddle getting cold. I don't think the Wallabies have cottoned onto that yet.

But when each team is supremely fit and strong (and warmed up), it's the top bit, the brain, which makes the difference between winning and losing.

As the NZ Rugby webpages explain:

"Haka is not merely a pastime of the Māori but was also a custom of high social importance in the welcoming and entertainment of visitors." And "Its mystique has evolved along with the fierce determination, commitment and high level skill which has been the hallmark of New Zealand's National game".

While these days it's treated by the public as a well-oiled part of the entertainment, many will recall from test matches in days gone by an All Black haka can be pretty "in-your-face" for the opposition.

To an opposing team who have never heard of Ngati Toa Chieftain Te Rauparaha and his story, Ka Mate can take the meaning of "Hey there, look at us. We're a cohesive group, confident and proud. And by the way, we're big and strong, and we're going to beat you!"

Despite what the relevant experts might say about its "welcoming" cultural message and the precision of the "dance", to an outsider a haka performed by a bunch of hairy 120 kg athletes is always going to be intimidating. That's even without the throat-slitting version.

If you were going to be effective in psyching-out your opposition, then intimidation is exactly what you are after.

In what is essentially a physical match-up, a show of unity and aggression matters when you are trying to get a mental advantage over the other team. That part of the game is what the spectators are there to see and it's what the All Blacks' haka puts on show.

On the other hand, if haka is designed to be a friendly welcome and not intimidating, then our sports teams ought to look at something else that is. Something that really puts the frighteners into the opponents.

Perhaps they could borrow some books and wave them around in front of the opposition?

Apparently waving a book around counts as intimidation in Aotearoa these days. Especially if the book waver is a mother of two and her adversary is a middle-aged man. How frightening!

Parliament is a competition; a match between those in government and those trying to get there.

Unlike rugby, it should not be an opportunity for entertainment despite how media like to portray it, and despite the ploys and antics of some "players".

I don't think the public want to be entertained by elected members on either side, in a tit-for-tat parliamentary contest at the tax-payers' expense.

An appropriate haka might satisfy both sides if they are keen to gain a psychological edge, but in the warm up, not during the game.

Building communities or building fences?

As a young man I spent a couple of European summers living in the Netherlands from where I raced my bicycle around the Continent. It was a great time, as I loved the long summer days in that cycling-centric place, and I liked the people with their forthright way of discussing things. Not surprisingly, I now have a good handful of friends of Dutch heritage here in the Manawatū.

One thing about the people in the Netherlands is that they are not shy in exposing the innards of their houses. With little or no front fence and huge front windows, their dwellings were designed to hide nothing. The bigger the house, the bigger the window through which you couldn't help but peer into - a usually tidy living space with ornaments, pictures, and comfortable chairs. You'd even see the occupants going about their business - at least that business normally associated with a living room.

Some people would even eat their meals in front of the window, so outsiders could see what they are eating. You try not to be nosy and look, but you do, and I'm sure they know.

There doesn't seem to be a singular reason provided for this form of Dutch openness, but at least one historian links it back to the Dutch reformation where Calvinistic doctrine preached staid morality and eschewal of material possessions. So, to show their neighbours that they had nothing to hide in relation to their possession or actions, the Dutch built big windows and left the curtains open.

While the rigid conservatism of that religious era in the Netherlands has shrunk over 400 years, the windows have grown to exemplify the openness of the Dutch.

With the penchant of the Dutch for sharing their abodes in mind, I'm a bit miffed about the current Palmerston North predilection for constructing towering front fences. Many of these fences are so high that you can't even see if a house is there, let alone whether it has a front window.

Where there were once small picket front fences or hedges marking the

115

front of a well-manicured lawn, there is now an ugly treated timber or fibro fence reaching to the sky.

So why is this happening? What do Palmerston Northerners have to hide?

Maybe some are planning for success of the Green's cannabis bill and have already planted some pots with pot, like the Dutch I guess. Or maybe they are into nude sunbathing, like the Dutch, although with our wind chill factor there'd be goose bumps galore.

Perhaps their teenage boys inhabit the front bedroom with the window, and no one wants to see that. I'd be building a fence too!

Or maybe, in contrast to the Calvinists, the good burgers of our town just don't want anyone to see what they've got or what they do. They just don't like sticky beaks or nosey Parkers. It's their call I guess, but it makes our streets look like ugly alleyways, uninviting, and uninteresting. It also voids any opportunity to interact with the householder as they work their front garden.

Building fences does the opposite of building community. And community is the thing that got us through the lockdowns, and is going to get us through the next few years.

So, when it comes to fences, let's go Dutch!

Where have all the urinals
gone? Ah, the well-being
of the individual!

Now, in the mens' public toilets, where once there was a stainless-steel wall above a drain, there are now only wall-mounted ceramic bowls each separated by a screen. The other side of the toilet facility is much the same as it used to be, although the cubicles for sit-down business now are bigger and don't seem to contain the "colourful" graffiti of days gone by.

During rush hour, cheek by cheek the stainless steel set up would get you two blokes per linear metre doing their business. Now with the ceramic bowls you get less than one; a great loss of efficiency. So the cubicles get appropriated for purposes not requiring a closed door, putting someone who really does need to sit down in a real bother. In that rush period the cubicles get messy, the paper runs out, queues form, and tempers fray.

The big stainless steel walls, now as rare as a country racecourse, had a lot going for them.

Occasionally you would come across the Art-Deco urinal with ceramic units and colourful tiles instead of stainless - beautifully constructed and really a work of art. Taking a piss back a hundred years ago was meant to be an experience.

You couldn't miss hitting a vast wall of steel, so mess was minimal. But now the modern bowls are set at various heights and have various shapes, so the really short or the really tall need to aim high and low, else there'll be spray. And spray drift is not something you want in the mens'.

I remember having to lift my young sons up while they did their pee into the ceramic, and that invariably ended up with their shirt around their neck, pants around their ankles, and a wet patch. Wouldn't have happened with the stainless steel wall.

What's more, the little hole at the bottom of the modern ceramic bowl seems to easily block with hair and other bits, so unless they are regularly cleaned one "station" quickly goes out of action, worsening the peak hour rush.

So what's the deal with the modern urinals?

There must be "experts", 'Urinary Architects' perhaps, who have come up with these designs. And for what reasons?

Is it because stainless steel has become too expensive? Perhaps modern mans' pee is more corrosive? Maybe men are such a good "aim" these days that spray is not an issue?

Or maybe in today's world a bit more privacy is necessary to effectively do your business?

Often now there isn't even a 'Mens'. Instead there are genderless toilets which are used by anyone. Granted, they're more socially acceptable, more comfortable, and able to cater for the needs of all and sundry. And they give you the seclusion to do other necessary stuff too like changing clothes or nappies. Some of them even have music!

However, each of these take up so much room that you could fit ten blokes in that same space if it had a stainless steel urinal.

I was travelling with my elderly father one day, and like many older men, the urge to pee came on fairly quickly. We got to the next town, stopped the car, and found a public toilet. It had three 'genderless' rooms, and quite a queue - almost exclusively younger women.

By then my dad didn't have the extra five or six minutes to wait for the next vacancy, even if one of the women in the queue had noticed an elderly gentleman in trouble and let him in.

In the old days, I'd have just asked the blokes to shuffle along and make room standing up along the stainless. Those blokes would have just moved along with an acknowledging nod and let my dad in.

In the end we shuffled off beside the dunny to do his thing there whilst I shielded him from the chattering queues.

My dad lost his dignity that day.

Someone should be starting a petition to 'bring back mens' urinals', so blokes can do their stuff quickly and efficiently without fuss. And people like my father can be catered for as well.

But in today's world where well-being of the individual trumps communal commonsense that'd be pissing into the wind...

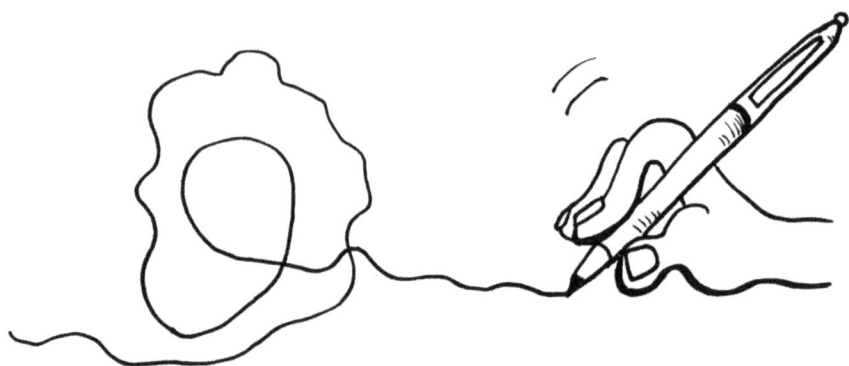

Self-Image and Positivity

Choose your parents wisely

The Yellow Beetle

Who turned the lights off twelve years ago?

Who are you?

Don't judge a person by what they do for a living

A top tier volunteer

Dropping the ego and realizing we can't always be right

Hair today, gone tomorrow

Choose your parents wisely

Some years ago the University of NSW created a special course for gifted children of school age. If through application the school decided that your child was "gifted" then they were invited to attend these special courses, at considerable cost.

There they would have the opportunity to stimulate their gifts and get further ahead than they would do if they only attended their regular school with regular children. They would also get branded with a "gifted" title, which some parents would no doubt enjoy, especially if they felt that their child's achievements reflected upon them.

Like most parents, I'm quietly confident all my kids are gifted - they take after their mother after all. So I would have been quite pleased to have them publicly labelled "gifted" had I been flush with money, had we been in NSW, and had they passed the entrance "test".

Anyway, the course organisers are hardly likely to turn paying customers away if they are just Miss Jane Average or Master John Median, especially if the Average and Median households have bigger incomes than their surnames would suggest.

What a great business model! Nearly as good as being the purveyor of an addictive substance like coffee!

So are you buying your kids a moniker, a reputation, or a future, that in the eyes of some perhaps they might not deserve? Only in America or Aussie surely, not here in good ole' egalitarian NZ?

Wrong.

Sport is the obvious local example. When my wife once asked my daughter's swim squad coach, "How do you identify talent?", without hesitation the coach quipped "wealthy parents". Very astute. Firstly, because any good coaching business is likely to tell the parents their child has talent and needs to keep coming back for coaching, and by the way, keep the monthly automatic payments flowing. Secondly, because getting to the top in just about any sport requires money. Entry fees, coaching, equipment, travel costs, sails, hay.... Some sports more than others of course, but very few of our gold medal winners come from poor families.

We are told that the best way to ensure a child's future is that they get a degree - leads to higher earning power and a certain status that those without will never have. But increasingly money talks in education too.

In my experience and especially over the past few years, NZ tertiary education providers have recently been pretty flexible to potential customers when it comes to academic entry standards.

Domestic students can sign up for most degrees with no deposit, interest free for three years – Ts and Cs apply of course. You just need to - if you have satisfactory marks from school - or be older than 20. Pretty much anyone can get a degree provided they pass, pass, pass, and then pay.

From the education providers' point of view, international students are gold. Those students fork out three times as much and upfront. They do have to be able to converse/write in English to a minimum standard, but it means NZ pretty much only get overseas students from wealthy families. So long as they pay, pay, pay, then pass.

Things have changed a bit recently with COVID19. International student fees, which provided nearly 20% of the average university income over the past decade or so, have all but dried up. That business model, one addicted to overseas full-fed-paying students, will be in a deep financial hole for a few years at least. They will have to come up with another gold mine. Schools for gifted NZ children perhaps?

In the end, you're not going to get that top job or gold medal without a bit of innate ability, hard work, and a bit of luck. But money makes hard work feel a little easier, and it certainly makes you luckier.

So kids, choose your parents and their pay packets wisely.

The Yellow Beetle

When my children were old enough to learn to drive we bought a small car, a manual, something that was fairly safe, hopefully reliable, and that wouldn't owe us anything after a few years of gearbox crunching.

It was yellow, not by choice, but because it was genuinely hard to find a manual car of the desired brand within our price range, and subsequently canary was all we could get.

Six years later the kids have gone but the car remains. It's our runabout, sometimes costing a bit to get a WOF, but otherwise useful when I need four wheels. I often use it when my other set of (four) wheels breaks down.

The other day I drove across town to a friend's place, and when I pulled up he said dead pan "I wouldn't be seen dead in a car like that". Seriously? I'm thinking, "What's wrong with a middle-aged bloke like me driving a bright yellow Beetle?", but he was not a fan.

It's never worried me what I drive as long as it gets me safe and dry from point A to point B without costing too much.

Car companies, however, want you to believe that the car maketh the man. Their marketing plans revolve around this. Drive a Ranger and you'll automatically know how to tow a boat, even if you don't have one. Drive a Hilux and a freezer full of venison is only a gun-shot away. Drive a Beamer and you'll become a successful real estate agent. Drive a Roller and you might just be related to the Queen.

This is partly why it's so hard to get people onto bicycles. It's not just because they are too lazy to ride, it's because many of us have been sucked in by car marketing which fools us into believing that the car we drive defines us. And when it does we certainly won't go across town without it.

A bicycle hardly has the same effect.

The flip side to the car manufacturers' marketing angle is that many people, like my friend, will judge others by what sort of car they drive.

You see a bloke in a suit driving a glossy black V8 and he must be rich. A woman with dark glasses driving a red two-door is obviously a corporate executive, and a bloke driving a people-mover is a Polynesian fruit-picker. Never mind that the suit needs to use credit to fill the tank, the woman is actually a car mechanic, and the Polynesian - a List MP on the hustings.

I think it's pretty sad if you gauge someone by what they drive. Didn't Martin Luther King say that, "We will one day live in a nation where they will not be judged by the colour of their car, but by the content of their character". Or something like that.

I still don't know what a yellow Beetle might say to others about the driver, but given my friend's reaction I can understand why my 19-year-old son didn't want to drive it to work.

My other car is an old green Land Rover.

Who turned the lights off twelve years ago?

I caught a whiff the other day of a long lost odour. Smells from the past powerfully evoke memories, and this one took me back to my teenage years.

It was the smell of stale male sweat, the smell that permeates a male changing room in the hours after training or a match.

It's not a pleasant smell by any means, but it took me straight back to my teenage years at school playing football and doing PE.

The teen years are, as most men admit, ones of anxiety of the body, pimples and hair, short and tall, voices breaking or not. And where girls are a different species prone to cutting remarks about boys but nevertheless beacons of their attention.

The once-a-week ordeal of getting into your PE gear in the boys' change room provided a yardstick of how close you were to being a man, or at least the "mature" boys in their final year. A quick glance around during changing or showering was confirmation of where you were in the developmental spectrum.

I recall that some fifteen-year-olds had chest hair and shaved every day whereas many, like me, still had unmown "bum-fluff" under their nose and little hair around the other bits. The size of the male appendage is similarly quite varied and largely follows developmental age.

The playing field evens out pretty quickly though, and by 18 pretty much everyone has cut their lip with a razor, has at least some hair in previously glabrous places, and suitably fills their Jockeys.

Of course, there were still some outliers who might have copped some flack, usually not the confident vigorous developers, but those behind the eight ball, especially if they still possessed a squeaky voice. But the latter guys grew up tough and without exception taller than the rest by their early 20s.

It's been a long time since I've showered in a smelly men's change room after a match or bike race, so I don't know what it's like now. But I suspect, given that we live in the era where individual comfort trumps efficiency, modern change rooms have showers with individual compartments, or shower curtains at least.

But seeing your peers in the nick is a sort of a right-of-passage for most blokes, because you discover that actually you are pretty normal - near the middle of the bell-curve - in most aspects of anatomy. Otherwise, how else would you know? Surely not from the internet, where steroid-enhanced abdominals and otherwise surgically enhanced bits of anatomy abound?

It's with some curiosity that, in the US, a charter school principal was forced to resign after year six students were shown pictures of Michelangelo's 'David.' Maybe it's because he has a penis? Or are his hands too big for the rest of his body? Only the School Board and complaining parents will know. Perhaps the latter turned the lights off at a critical time twelve years ago?

Are they also going to ban pictures of the magnificent ancient Greek 'Discobolus' (the 'Discus Thrower'), because he wasn't wearing pants either!

Either way, I'm not sure what that says about education in Florida or the USA in general, but since when did a naked human body become a no-go area in education?

Typically, the Italians have responded with incredulity accusing the American school of having, "no understanding of Western culture and not understanding Renaissance art".

I sincerely hope this sort of attitude is not happening here in NZ education. And I hope that teenage boys (and girls) get the chance to gauge their development in some safe way. Because the very vast majority will take comfort in learning that they are normal.

Granted, I write this from middle age, where your body starts deteriorating and a point after which you don't really care about what other people think about what you look like; with and without clothes. Your partner may be an exception, but even then physical attraction starts to become less important than a sense of humour.

In middle age taking a shower surrounded by a bunch of other similar-aged naked men after footy training isn't such an ordeal as it would have been as an anxious teenager. Post-match middle-age players would be far more worried about their knees, ankles, and who brought the beer for later.

I bet the change rooms still smell the same though.

Who are you?

I did another online survey the other day, this time for the IRD or some Govt Dept like that. Like most of these questionnaires, they finish off asking you how old you are, your gender, your ethnicity, and how much you earn.

I'm often inclined to lie - about my age in particular, then for some reason I think I'd better be truthful. Especially if I finish by providing my email to go in the draw for a first prize $100 Pak-N-Save voucher (or the second prize two nights in Rotorua).

The ethnicity question is the one that I have difficulty answering because it generally only has options for being Māori, Pacific, European, and Other. Sometimes there are extras like Asian, Tokeloan, Samoan, Fijian, Pakeha, and Kiwi. I was born in Australia, but have a NZ passport, so following the geographical lead of the options, the closest correct answer for me would be Pacific Islander. However, against my better judgement, I mostly tick the Euro box.

Ethnicity is not an easy subject to get your head around, even if we were to ignore the modern predilection for tying it to measures of all sorts. So, as usual, a quick trip to the Statistics NZ website provides some guidance.

Their definition is "...the ethnic group or groups that people identify with or feel they belong to." So, ethnicity is self-perceived, not what you look like, or what other people label you as being.

I have fairly pale skin, but I don't identify in any way as a European. People from there dress with style, are infatuated with soccer, kiss each other on both cheeks, take holidays in the South of Spain, drink red wine, and hate the English. On the other hand, I've never been to Spain, dress casually, and prefer beer. A single peck on the cheek is fine and I enjoy watching a game of Rugby League. Oh, and my wife has a British passport.

But what ethnic group do I come from? One not on that list.

Again, Statistics NZ gives us a clue, defining an ethnic group as a social group whose members have the following characteristics:

• share a sense of common origins

• claim a common and distinctive history and destiny

- possess one or more dimensions of collective cultural individuality
- feel a sense of unique collective solidarity.

Goodness, with the above in mind the closest social group I can relate to are cyclists. Cyclists all spend much time in a bike shop, all have a history of riding bikes, and coffee shops are our destiny. Cyclists certainly possess cultural individuality – look at the dress sense - and, against the hatred of motorists and stirring from the media, feel a sense of collective solidarity.

Of course that would mean someone who abuses me for riding is a racist. So when the bloke in the big ute winds down his window at the traffic lights and tells me to get off the effing road, I'll just smugly call him a racist. That'll learn him. And anyway, he'd more likely be prosecuted for that than if he ran me over with his Ford Predator.

In practice though, according to Statistics NZ, ethnicity is defined as the ethnic group or groups reported by respondents to the ethnic group question in the Census of Population and Dwellings and other Statistics New Zealand surveys.

Anyone who constructs surveys knows that you should not ask leading questions. Yet our ethnic identities are confined by the categories someone else has given us.

So, putting my scientist hat on, shouldn't my DNA provide the best answer for the ethnicity question?

About two years ago, before my father passed, I had he and my mum do one of those DNA tests. I thought it'd be interesting for them, and since my DNA is theirs, interesting for me to see what my heritage is.

There were always stories of course, oral history of the family, including that somewhere my mum had Jewish lineage and on my dad's side, plenty of Irish, and English from the Norfolk Broads.

While DNA-based geographical ancestry is a bit like bucket chemistry and is a moving feast depending on how many others have also done it, my family's oral history lined up with much of what the DNA threw up.

My dad's DNA was almost exactly one third Irish, one third Scottish, and one third English, though from Manchester and Isle of Man rather than the Broads.

My mum's DNA was more interesting and did indeed throw up a decent chunk of Jewish. With some detective work from one of my sisters and a cousin, I now know that my Jewish ancestry was Berber. My cousin has even now visited their "home" synagogue in Morocco. And except for one male along the line, I'd be a "formal" bona fide Jew.

Despite the weight of DNA evidence though, I still don't see myself as European.

Originating from the biggest island in the pacific and living in the second biggest, I'm a cycling South Pacific Islander with an ocker accent who is a kosher Kiwi and Jewish as.

Don't judge a person by what they do for a living

Often when filling in forms you are asked what you do for work; what your occupation is.

These days I have to think about what I actually do for a job because the hours in my day are spent during a variety of things.

I used to spend my working week as an academic so I once comfortably defined myself as that. The remuneration was fairly good and there is generally respect associated with the title of 'Professor', even in poppy-pruning NZ.

Nowadays, although I spend much of my time pulling coffee, cleaning tables, and washing up, I still behave like an academic in my way of thinking, probably in a more rounded way than before.

Many would dream to earn a PhD and become a professor. For some, being a tenured academic would be their pinnacle life vocation.

On the other hand, I don't reckon many people in NZ would aspire to coffee shop work, and I wonder how many baristas write that on their travel documents least they be judged by that.

So why keep doing barista work?

For me it's the positive influence I can have on people which keeps me doing the coffee thing in spite of the low pay and the deferential nature of the job. Whether it's seeing a customer leave the café happily caffeinated, providing a friendly ear, or making someone laugh, I feel like I can influence a person to make their day better in some small way.

To be a good barista, you also have to be able to quickly judge a customer when they walk in the door. Are they in a good mood, or a bad one, wanting some quiet time or just a quick caffeine hit? Do they want conversation, or "just the coffee thanks"? And of course, a barista has to be able to make a decent coffee.

Despite the skill required, here in NZ the job of a coffee shop worker is given the same vocational weighting as a cleaner or elderly care assistant.

The sorts of jobs that are seen as fill-ins; stuff you do while waiting for your dream job or studying for something else. Despite their importance they are not regarded as jobs for life.

Since when was the last time a barista was mentioned in the New Years' Honours list for services to the community? Plenty of big business people are, and their life's work has been to make money for themselves. Plenty of sports people are, and their goal because it absolutely has to be, is simply to beat the opposition.

It's no wonder we have staff shortages in nursing homes and hospitality venues, whereas we have an over-supply of people wanting to go into well-paid white-collar jobs or play for the All Blacks.

But does it have to be that way? No, and it's not that way in many other countries where the butcher, baker, and coffee-maker converse on equal terms with the local brain surgeon and resident rocket scientist.

In a perfect world the value of a job should be seen by the wider community primarily as how much you contribute to improving the lot of others. Not what you get paid, how many boards you've been on, or how many degrees you have.

I write the odd article for this newspaper not only because it helps me maintain my hard-earned writing skills, but because I like to think I can encourage readers to look at things from a different angle. That is, it's another way I can influence people in some positive way and make their day a little more interesting.

So nowadays when I'm filling in a form with a question, "What is your occupation?" I write down barista and influencer. Admittedly an ugly one with poor fashion sense who's never been to Bali, and who's pictorially challenged.

A top tier volunteer

Volunteers are gold. They are the underground army who do something, not for financial reward, but for a greater good or to help others, usually while providing some personal fulfillment.

Paying someone to do a job means that you can outline the nature of that job, instruct the tasks required, and call them to account if the work is not done properly. And paying someone in a job is like a retainer; even if they don't particularly enjoy the work, they will come back for more because they need the money.

Not so a volunteer who can walk away if the work becomes a drag.

Managing or directing a team of volunteers is a real skill. You need to be able to encourage/cajole them so that the work gets done, and then enable them to get sufficient satisfaction that they'll stick around and continue helping out. This involves respecting the volunteer and their time, and profuse thanks afterwards to indicate how much their effort is valued.

All too often though, volunteers are not respected or valued. Their work is not acknowledged and thankless.

The most common volunteer (unpaid) job in the world is being a full-time care-giver of a relative. Most of those are mums, and increasingly dads. Many full-time parents are also volunteers at school or sport or church, or look after the children of others after school where people in paid work don't have time. Full-time parents are the top tier of volunteers and they are gold.

Yet, our society seems to have been fooled into thinking that, if someone is not paid, their work has little value. And it follows that the more someone is paid, the higher their status and the more valuable we think the work that they do.

However, when you have a hard look at this, the reverse is mostly true.

People that are paid least are cleaners, early childhood workers, agricultural laborers, and nursing home staff. People that are paid most are senior executives, marketing gurus, and financial wizards. I would hazard a guess that we could do without many of the latter, but society would cease to function without the former. No one has yet been able to explain to me exactly what contribution a 'futures trader' makes to society for example, but they still make plenty of lolly.

International Women's Day was held recently, and amongst other things, it occasioned celebration of the achievements of noteworthy women.

Outstanding women, like men have been forever, were placed on a pedestal because they are paid a load of money to be directors, executives, high flyers, and tell other lesser paid people what to do. I guess someone's got to do it.

But not once in that time of women, or in the weeks since, have I seen acknowledgement of those doing the most important work of all; that of being a mum. And since when was being a dad put at the top of the totem pole? I s'pose there is Mothers' Day in a few months and Fathers' Day later on, but those events are commercial, not about elevating the societal value of primary care-givers or the value of their input to the community.

I fear that women and men are being strongly discouraged from aspiring to become full-time parents because little value is attached to it, and so it goes, little societal status. Instead they are being encouraged into roles for reasons little more than attached status which can then define them. Oh, and tick the 'mum' or 'dad' box if you want, but it's your career and status which is most important.

But the problem about being defined by the status of your job is that one day you won't have either. On the other hand, being a parent is a permanent position, poorly paid, but mostly fulfilling.

As my elderly German aunt used to say, "once a rooster, now a feather duster"; a description, obviously, for high-flying men past their prime. Modern men, and increasingly women, in their flight to the top roost would do well to take heed.

Dropping the ego and realizing we can't always be right

My wife and I sit down after dinner and do the Manawatu Standard quick crossword most evenings. She's better than me with words, so usually I'm the onlooker as she fills in the boxes. Sometimes though, I get on a roll and can knock over a good deal of it quickly. When you're hot you're hot, but with crosswords, mostly I'm not.

If she's not around I'll try to do it on my own. More often than not I fill in half a dozen of the words starting at the top left and then I get stuck. I can fill in 1-across and maybe 2- and 4-down and then I struggle a little with 6-across and so on.

So, I move down to other parts of the crossword and fill in a few words here and there, trying to link those so I can get a letter or two as a clue for the words I'm stuck on. Words that will fit or nearly fit in other spots fill my head and I develop a plan on how to go forward confident that what I've done to that point is correct. But I fill in the boxes lightly because something doesn't seem quite right.

There comes a critical point at which you have to admit to yourself you've gone wrong somewhere. That's when I generally lose interest and try to guess the nine-letter word in the Target puzzle.

Inevitably, my wife arrives, sits down next to me, and changes one word in my partially completed crossword to something else that fits the clue a bit better, and the rest of the puzzle falls into place. Essentially, I had one wrong word near the start and I was trying to make the rest fit in with that.

Sometimes that mistake was back at the beginning and then, because you've seen some way forward, you can get a long way before reality hits.

A similar scenario can play out in science. Many experts have taken their research activities down a particular route of investigation and ultimately hit a brick wall when, unbeknownst to them, their hypothesis or methodology was wrong to start with. The further they go down that incorrect road, or the more they've invested in that direction, the harder it is to recognise that critical point and realise the error of their way.

Many an ego has been bruised by this and I have seen ongoing academic argument when one research group will not accept rejection of their tightly held idea or hypothesis when someone else refutes it. Some scientists will spend the rest of their career trying to prove that they were right, when in fact they were not.

Very occasionally you hear of someone who has fiddled their data to make it fit a flawed hypothesis. Eventually those people get found out and discredited.

To admit defeat is to eat humble pie and admit that you were wrong. Reputations and egos are at stake, and being wrong doesn't pertain to continuation of grant funding. But a good and honest scientist or academic is able to admit their error and move on.

In this context, crosswords are easy; the answers are almost always 100% right or wrong. So, that critical point at which you can concede your mistake is obvious. Less so applied sciences like epidemiology, or public health, and even less so business where getting timely empirical (measured) data is often difficult.

Like a crossword it's really good to have two or more people, or two or more teams of experts, working on an important problem at the same time. It is ideal if they interpret each clue or data set differently, looking at it from a different viewpoint. Ideal if they disagree. Then, as a collective, they are covering the bases better, can discuss the results, and are less likely to go down the wrong path and hold tight to an idea that might not be quite right in the first place.

If, in the end, if both parties were found to be wrong, sharing the humble pie is a lot more palatable than eating the whole thing on your own!

Hair today, gone tomorrow

November is when it's trendy to grow a moustache. It doesn't matter what it looks like because it's for a good cause. Any mo is acceptable in Nov, but not during other months of the year.

There are good mos and bad ones. Good ones make you look like Errol Flynn or Tom Selleck. Bad ones make you look like Augusto Pinochet or Snidely Whiplash.

Some blokes can grow a good mo overnight, where others could spend all November trying and still look like they are just hitting puberty.

The only time I grew a moustache it made me look like a porn star. Or a policeman from Melbourne.

I can do a reasonable fist of the goatie beard/mo combo. However, the full Ned Kelly is well beyond my hirsute ability because my facial hair doesn't grow much on my cheeks. Lucky I wasn't an adult in the 70s when sideburns were worn to work to accompany shorts and long socks.

I'd like to try a handlebar moustache, but I'm too short and my motorbike is Japanese.

For some people, hair is a big part of who they are and they become quite attached to it. Consequently, many spend a lot of time and considerable money on their hair.

I can especially appreciate the effort and resources required for nicely managed head hair on a woman especially when it's long and thick.

Lots of blokes though take their hair very seriously too. Product every day and beards trimmed daily within an inch of their life.

After losing mine twice with chemo I've pretty much decided that hair is overrated.

In fact, having almost no body hair makes a shower a breeze. It's a great way of saving hot water and shampoo. Everyone should try it, but I don't recommend getting rid of hair in the same way I did.

To many, well managed hair might indicate a well-managed and successful life, but not always. Look at Einstein.

You need to be careful about judging a person through their hair because hair can come unstuck for many reasons. Age, disease, accidents, bad management, or just being a man.

I tell my wife that it must be easier being a woman when it comes to hair. Few women lose their head hair whereas many men do. Women don't have to shave their face each day and don't grow hair out of their nose or their ears (do they?). And I'm assuming most don't have hair on their chest.

Being a bloke on the other hand comes with all sorts of hairy trouble. What woman has ever cut her upper lip shaving? Or missed a bit on her chin and only realized when looking in the bus window on the way to work.

And try putting sunscreen on hairy male arms and legs. You go through litres of the stuff. It's primarily why cyclists shave their legs, not because of aerodynamics.

Then there are blokes who have a thick carpet of hair on their shoulders and back. They'd need to be sponsored by a sunscreen manufacturer to get through summer.

Sadly, hairy backs are pas acceptable these days and many men are encouraged to shave their torso hair off. But perhaps once upon a time it was useful. Channeling Charles Darwin, maybe it kept their female partners warm in winter so they could pass on their thick back hair genes? Maybe stone-age women adored it, otherwise why has it remained in the human genome?

Here's a thought. We could have 'Back Hair Month' in support of something like sunscreen use. That would make those of the hirsute torso trendy for at least part of the year, and our sunscreen makers would make a killing.

About the Writer
Steve Stannard

Stephen was born in Mildura, a typical large Aussie town (now city) in country Victoria, just across the border from NSW in 1967. He spent his first few years on an agricultural research station, where his father worked as an agricultural scientist. Although the family moved to Sydney when Steve was just four, he always remained at heart, a "country boy".

Growing up in Sydney's Eastwood in the '70's, Steve's was a typical Aussie suburban childhood - cricket down the driveway, building billycarts and hunting for tadpoles in the local creek. Steve and his sisters (two older, two younger) attended the local Eastwood Primary School, where Steve was school captain in 1978.

From there he went to the "selective" James Ruse Agricultural High School, long known for being the highest academically ranked high school in Australia. He loved the practical agricultural lessons and embraced the intellectual challenge. During his high school years Steve also grew a love of outdoor adventure from his scouting activities. He and his best mate took on the Hawkesbury Canoe Classic, a 111kms race, several times. From school he attended Sydney University, where he studied Agricultural Science. He continued with his kayaking, attempting the much more challenging solo Murray River Challenge – a five-day 415km race! During training, and thanks to a wrist injury, he was forced onto the bike to maintain his fitness, which led to his first cycle race, a time-trial near Penrith NSW - which of course he won. The rest, as they say, is history.

Although still a country boy at heart, he'd spent most of his life in the city and so felt a little out of place amongst his farming graduate mates. So on finishing university, instead of taking on an agricultural job, he set off to race his bike in Europe. These were in the Pro/Am days, and Steve raced as an amateur in Belgium and The Netherlands for a number of seasons. He loved the Dutch countryside and the people and was billeted by several families. This was also the era of the "druggy days" with metaphors such as "Belgian Pin-cushions" and "Vitamins" - it was difficult to know who would be going well in which race, depending on who had taken what in the hours beforehand.

139

Steve returned home disillusioned about European cycling, but having particularly loved the experiences he gained from cycle touring.

Back in Sydney, Steve continued to train and race his bike at a national and international level whilst working part-time in the local post office. He represented Australia in the Tour of Dubai and was 10th in the Commonwealth Bank Classic - the first major stage race in the Oceania region. The quality of this race was such that in that year, it was won by a 19-year-old Jan Ulrich, who would go on to win the Tour de France and become World Champion.

Steve met Katherine (who was also a cyclist) and decided that it might be time to knuckle down. He completed a Masters degree in Nutrition at Sydney University, where his final project brought him into contact with the School of Exercise and Sports Science. From there it was a short step to a PhD – well, a short step to starting a PhD. By the time Steve had finished his PhD, he had a wife and three children! Next stop Palmerston North, New Zealand and Massey University where he started as an exercise physiology lecturer.

Not sure what Massey were expecting when they employed Steve, but if they were looking for someone bursting with energy and ideas, with an incredible work ethic, staunch scientific integrity and who was never satisfied with the status quo, then they got exactly what they wanted. Steve had only a relatively short time at Massey, 16 years, but during that time he not only rose to be Head of the newly formed School of Sport, but also travelled widely to conferences and to collaborate with international colleagues. He published profusely (over 150 papers, which have in turn been cited over 6,000 times), in top-of-the-line publications. He built and mentored a core team of academics and PhD students and created a school which was humming with innovation and novel research.

During this time, of course, Steve was also father to three active young children. Weekends were spent zooming from one sporting event to the next – soccer in the morning and in the afternoon, cross-country running (winter) triathlon (summer) with road biking on Saturday, mountain biking on Sunday. Phew! With their youngest just 11, Steve and Katherine took the crew cycle touring in Europe. Amsterdam to Strasbourg, 1,200km in a little under three weeks! The family crew aptly named themselves, the "Stannard Train".

Steve's time in academia all started to come apart following several poor decisions by Massey management, and by 2015 he was thinking about a Plan B for his life and career. He decided that vertical integration was the way to go, looking to start a small business that people couldn't bypass by going on line. So in 2016 "Cyclista" a coffee bar in George Street, Palmerston North, was born. As Steve's career as a small business owner started, he was also diagnosed with multiple myeloma. It was during the last eight years that Steve not only built a small business from scratch, but also conceived and ran the internationally prestigious Gravel and Tar professional cycle race - the only single-day UCI (Union Cycliste Internationale) race in New Zealand - which built a reputation as being the "toughest one-day cycling event in the Oceania region".

Despite the cancer challenge, Steve made two more cycle touring trips to Europe with Katherine. During this time, he used all his exercise physiology expertise and contacts to fight the UCI and defend his son against (ridiculous and unfounded) accusations of blood doping.

He used his hard won teaching skills to write and have published over 80 opinion pieces on a wide range of topics including the community, politics, the environment, business, education, health – in fact just about every issue or topic that was of concern to the community at the time. A selection of these – many of which are still relevant today - are contained in this book. Plus, he got up seven mornings a week at 5:30am to bake scones, muffins and his legendary banana bread for the Cyclista Café.

Steve lived as if he didn't have a moment to waste – and he didn't waste a moment...

Acknowledgements

The following are gratefully acknowledged for their contributions for enabling this book to be published:

Matthijs van Wagtendonk

John and Michelle van Lienen

Leigh Greer

Lizzy Kent

Rob Baan

Rowena Baan-Mathias

John Waldon

Grant Smith, PNCC Mayor

Ross Hyde

John and Joanne Stewart

Ray Geor

Etech NZ Ltd

Malcolm Bailey

Ann Jarden

Bob Selden

Anita Derks

Jeremy McGuire

Ben Odering

Tanya Little

Steve Davey

Gary King

The Greasy Chain Charitable Trust